3 1457 00002 6154

W9-BFS-851

Treasures from Europe

WITHDRAWN

New Canaan Library
151 Main Street
New Canaan, CT 06840

(203) 594-5000
www.newcanaanlibrary.org

SEP 1 4 2004

Treasures from Europe

Stories and Classroom Activities

Flora Joy

2003
Teacher Ideas Press
Libraries Unlimited
A Member of Greenwood Publishing Group, Inc.
Westport, Connecticut

J
372.5
J

Copyright © 2003 Flora Joy
All Rights Reserved
Printed in the United States of America

No part of this publication may be reproduced, stored in a retrieval system, or transmitted, in any form or by any means, electronic, mechanical, photocopying, recording, or otherwise, without the prior written permission of the publisher. An exception is made for individual librarians and educators, who may make copies of activity sheets for classroom use in a single school or library. Standard citation information should appear on each page.

Teacher Ideas Press
LIBRARIES UNLIMITED
A Member of Greenwood Publishing Group, Inc.
88 Post Road West
Westport, CT 06881
1-800-225-5800
www.lu.com

Library of Congress Cataloging-in-Publication Data

ISBN 1-56308-963-7

This work is dedicated to my handsome, clever, charming, delightful, intelligent, patient, warm, loving, exciting, daring, caring, and all-around perfect husband, Henry Joy, III.

Contents

Part II—CHALLENGE STORIES

Foreword

Stories and folk literature as an element of culture provide insight into other elements of that culture. Its indication of values within a culture provides readers (listeners) with the opportunity to learn about the culture. However, understanding and appreciating folk literature also requires knowledge of factors influencing the culture represented by that literature. At a minimum, this knowledge must include historical, geographic, and linguistic elements.

As Flora Joy developed this book, she and the section authors provided both background information and follow-up information and activities designed to enable readers (listeners) to obtain the knowledge that will place the stories into the appropriate cultural framework. They have also provided some examples of words (including meanings and pronunciations) of the languages used in the literature. It is beyond the scope of this publication, however, to provide full information on the language represented by any piece of writing or to provide complete descriptions of the history, geography, or other elements that interact with the aspects of culture represented in a given work. She hopes that these stories stimulate readers or listeners to learn more about the represented cultures and to extend the practice to stories of other cultures and subcultures.

The stories included in this book represent only a small sample of our world's cultures. Readers (listeners) are encouraged to reflect on their own culture and to make comparisons with the cultures represented by the selected literature. A factor that will surely strike many readers is the similarity of values across the diverse cultures.

The commonality of values among cultures creates a special problem for the collectors and presenters of folk literature. Joy used collectors and tellers whose backgrounds provided first-hand experiences with the cultures represented by their stories. Although this procedure can produce a story that represents the culture of a specific region or country, it does not mean that everyone in that country shares exactly that same culture. As readers examine their own culture, they will recognize differences in cultural elements within classes, schools, neighborhoods, and even families. Some of these differences are parallel to language, which is so interwoven with culture that separating the two is sometimes impossible. There are languages (generally observable as different from each other and logically recognized as equals), dialects (varieties of language usually associated with a geographic region or a social group), and idiolects (the varieties of a language as spoken by separate individuals). Culture parallels language; subculture parallels dialect; and self-culture or individual culture parallels idiolect.

The countries from which the stories in this book are drawn are typically smaller than the United States in both area and population. Most also are older than U.S. cultures, with the exception of the Native Americans. Their people are likely to be more similar than Americans. Yet they will still vary.

The ultimate goals are greater understanding and appreciation of cultural elements and greater tolerance for differences. These goals apply within our culture and in comparison to the cultures represented in the stories.

—Dr. John M. Taylor, III
Professor Emeritus of Reading, Linguistics, and Research
East Tennessee State University

How to Use This Book

Purpose

The purpose of this book is to provide material for storytellers, teachers, and librarians that will entice listeners to explore cultures other than their own. Folk literature helps tell the story of the people in the culture. These stories, therefore, can be used as an avenue for cultural exploration in classrooms or with listening audiences.

Organization

This book is organized into nine sections. The final two sections are intended to be a special challenge for all presenters and learners. All sections have a divider page, a page of information about the section contributor, background material, the cultural story, follow-up information, and questions pertaining to the story, the cultural background, or both.

Divider Page

The book includes divider pages to provide both a visual separation sheet between sections and a cover page for educators who wish to prepare duplicated packets for student use. It gives the story title, the country or region of the culture, and a map. The map shows the country or region as a separate division of the world, and it depicts the geographic location of this region in relation to the entire world. Learners who may be unfamiliar with the culture or country may therefore envision the locale of the culture on a world map.

Page About Section Contributor

Each page gives a brief biographical sketch and photograph of the individual who was primarily responsible for the preparation of the section.

Background Material

Prior to reading or telling the story, the presenter may prepare listeners by providing needed or desired information. For most sections, more information is provided than may be needed. Presenters of this material are encouraged to study the background section carefully. After analyzing the listeners' needs, ages, desires, and interests, carefully select that which would be appropriate during the presentation time. The following suggestions are made for this background material:

- If a **glossary** is provided, become familiar with the pronunciation and meanings of the words until you are able to pronounce them with ease. Decide which of these words should be introduced to the listeners and then cleverly present them before telling the story. Don't make this a formal lesson. Instead, introduce the necessary words in an interesting context. All words in these glossaries do not have to be "taught." They are there primarily for the presenter's benefit.

- Some sections contain **reproducible pages** for student use. Decide which of these pages would be of benefit to the listeners. These may be copied and distributed for discussion purposes to establish an appropriate mind-set for the upcoming story.

- **Additional cultural information** is given in most sections. The presenter should read this to determine which ideas and concepts should be explained to listeners prior to the story presentation. This information should be shared in an interesting and exciting manner instead of as a lecture or mere listing of facts.

The Story

Stories in these sections are from one to four pages in length. They may be told or read to the listeners. An alternative to storytelling or story reading would be to provide printed copies of the story for the learners to read independently.

The Follow-Up Material

A variety of follow-up material is provided in these sections. As with the background portion, these follow-up pages may be used in various ways. Some may be duplicated for individual responses, others may be used for discussion purposes, and several are intended for additional presenter information.

Wrap-Up Activity

Unit closure for the first seven stories in this book is offered through an activity called "Game Show Fun." A separate description is provided for this exercise.

The Challenge

The two final stories in this book are presented as a special challenge. Except for lacking the final "Game Show Fun" section, they have an identical format to that of the first seven. These two stories will present a challenge both to the adult presenter and to learners. They are more difficult to tell because of specific cultural words from the original text. Instead of being folktale adaptations (like the stories in the first seven sections), one is a true personal story, and the other is an oral history tale, based on real happenings. Also, in lieu of the "Game Show" questions (also presented in the first seven sections), these two stories have numerous thought-provoking questions for which there are no "correct" answers. They are meant to challenge listeners and to promote continued thinking—long after the story has been told and the questions discussed—about the issues presented. Instructional leaders may use these questions in any manner that best fits the needs of the target audience.

A Final Thought

All audiences, libraries, and classrooms are unique. The material in this book is designed to offer the presenter a wide variety of choices for different types of listening groups. Be as innovative as possible with the information provided, and always keep the *enjoyment* in the listening and learning process. Have fun!

Game Show Fun

The first seven stories in this book all have a set of fifteen questions at the end of the section. These questions may be used in a variety of ways for interesting, challenging, and motivating follow-up activities. It is strongly suggested that the questions be used for fun experiences rather than as a "test" of the content. The failure to recall a specific fact from a story should not "subtract points" from a learner's grade for the day. Instead, the questions could be used for group fun.

Adult leaders are limited only by their imaginations for how to use these questions. Here are some examples:

- If game show formats from television programs are used, for example, a three-column "Jeopardy" board could be prepared.

- If questions are placed on separate cards, teams of students could have a "quick challenge" of who could provide the correct answer first. The correct responder receives the card, and the student who accumulates the highest number of cards is "the winner." In this case, the correct answers could be written on the backs of the cards.

- The adult leader could read the question stem for each question. Volunteers may provide possible answers, with correct responses rewarded as appropriate for the group.

Proceed with these questions in any desirable manner for the listeners involved, keeping in mind that *fun* should be among the goals.

Answers for "Game Show Fun" Questions

Answers to *A Treasure for Anders* questions: 1 = C, 2 = A, 3 = D, 4 = B, 5 = A, 6 = A, 7 = C, 8 = D, 9 = B, 10 = C, 11 = A, 12 = A, 13 = D, 14 = C, 15 = D.

Answers to *The Three Reeds* questions: 1 = C, 2 = B, 3 = D, 4 = A, 5 = B, 6 = A, 7 = B, 8 = A, 9 = C, 10 = D, 11 = A, 12 = D, 13 = B, 14 = C, 15 = D.

Answers to *The Lorelei* questions: 1 = D, 2 = B, 3 = C, 4 = D, 5 = A, 6 = C, 7 = B, 8 = C, 9 = A, 10 = B, 11 = D, 12 = D, 13 = D, 14 = B, 15 = D.

Answers to *Clever Peter and the Sultan* questions: 1 = B, 2 = A, 3 = D, 4 = C, 5 = B, 6 = A, 7 = D, 8 = B, 9 = B, 10 = C, 11 = A, 12 = D, 13 = B, 14 = C, 15 = C.

Answers to *Pacala* questions: 1 = C, 2 = D, 3 = A, 4 = D, 5 = B, 6 = A, 7 = A, 8 = C, 9 = D, 10 = B, 11 = A, 12 = C, 13 = A, 14 = D, 15 = D.

Answers to *Gilitrutt* questions: 1 = D, 2 = B, 3 = A, 4 = C, 5 = D, 6 = A, 7 = D, 8 = D, 9 = C, 10 = C, 11 = C, 12 = A, 13 = B, 14 = D, 15 = D.

Answers to *Nasreddin Odjah's Clothes* questions: 1 = D, 2 = B, 3 = C, 4 = A, 5 = D, 6 = A, 7 = D, 8 = B, 9 = C, 10 = C, 11 = D, 12 = B, 13 = A, 14 = D, 15 = C.

I
Folktales

Chapter 1

A Treasure for Anders

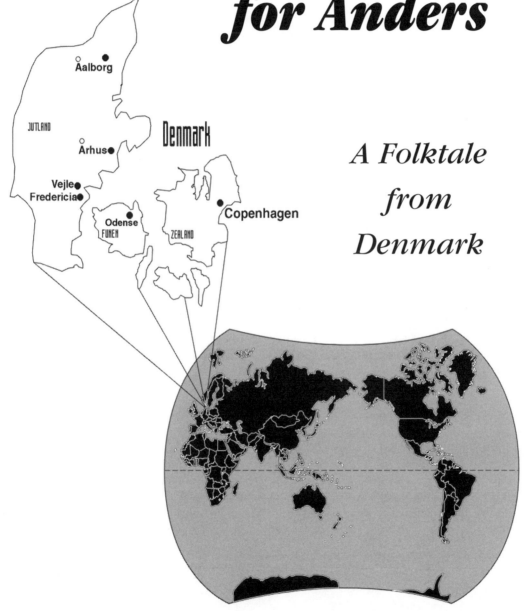

A Folktale from Denmark

About the Contributor

This section was prepared primarily by

Roger Petersen

Roger Petersen's grandparents were born in Denmark and immigrated to the United States as adults. His Danish heritage motivated him to engage in an intensive study of the customs, language, history, and folklore of Denmark. He has traveled throughout Denmark exploring both the culture and the life of his favorite storyteller, Hans Christian Andersen. In 2002 Roger was the only American storyteller to perform at the International Hans Christian Andersen Conference in Salt Lake City, Utah.

Roger is a professional educator, humorist, and storyteller. In these capacities he has addressed audiences throughout the United States and Canada. He is an honors graduate of Philadelphia Biblical University, Trinity International University, and East Tennessee State University, where he received a master's degree in story arts. He is presently an associate professor of speech and story performance at Philadelphia Biblical University, where he has taught since 1982. He is a senior instructor with Walk Thru the Bible Ministries and is consistently recognized as one of the organization's top presenters. He has told the story of the entire Bible to more than 90,000 at more than 550 gatherings.

A Treasure for Anders (Denmark)—Cultural Background

Before exploring Danish culture through the story *A Treasure for Anders,* information about Denmark should be reviewed. The following areas may be selected as desired for such a review.

NOTABLE FACTS ABOUT DENMARK

- The name Denmark (*Danmark* in Danish), which means "field of the Danes," is more than a thousand years old. The name, as well as the kingdom, is the oldest in Europe.

- There are more bicycles than people in Denmark, and there are twice as many bicycles as cars.

- Denmark has the highest standard of living in all the European Community, and its citizens pay the highest taxes of any people in the world.

- Denmark publishes more books per capita than any other nation in the world and has a literacy rate of more than 99 percent.

- Candle making is an ancient trade in Denmark and is also one of the many modern examples of the Danish gift for combining form and function. Danes love candles and will even burn them at breakfast.

- Each year on the Fourth of July, American Independence Day is celebrated in Denmark at the Rebild National Park near Åalborg.

- So active was Danish resistance during the closing years of World War II that only fifty-three Danish Jews lost their lives in the European Holocaust.

NATIONAL DATA FOR DENMARK
(According to a 1994 census)

Population: 5,200,000

Capital: Copenhagen (1,339,000)

Other large cities: Århus (258,000); Odense (174,000); and Åalborg (155,000)

Government: A multiparty constitutional monarchy with one legislative house

Official language: Danish (The most frequently spoken foreign languages are English, followed by German.)

Official religion: Lutheranism

Religious affiliations: Lutheran: 90.6%; Roman Catholic: 0.5%; Jewish: 0.1%; others: 8.8%

Ethnic composition: Danish: 97.2%; Turkish: 0.5%; other Scandinavians: 0.4%; others: 1.9%

Life expectancy: Male: 73 years; Female: 78 years

Official name: Kingdom of Denmark

Land area: 16,633 square miles

Density: 206 people per square mile

Distribution: Urban: 87%; Rural: 13%

DANISH GEOGRAPHY

With a land area of 16,633 square miles, Denmark is the smallest and southernmost of the Scandinavian countries. It consists of the peninsula of Jutland (*Jylland*) that extends two hundred miles north from the German border, the two main islands of Zealand (*Sjælland*) and Funen (*Fyn*), and nearly five hundred other islands of which more than one hundred are inhabited.

Denmark has an irregular coastline of more than 4,500 miles. No one in Denmark lives more than thirty miles from the ocean.

The temperature ranges from an average of 33°F in January to 63°F in July. The North Atlantic Drift warms Denmark's cool but temperate climate.

The Danish landscape is varied but mostly flat. Denmark averages only about 100 feet above sea level. The highest "mountain" in Denmark is only 482 feet above sea level. The Danes call this point *Himmelbjerget* (Sky Mountain), evidence of the Dane's delightful sense of humor.

DANISH FARMS AND FARMING

Denmark's level terrain has always been suited to farming, which even today accounts for more than two-thirds of Denmark's land area. The soil in Eastern Jutland (where the story *A Treasure for Anders* takes place) is particularly fertile. At the time of this folktale and up through the life of Hans Christian Andersen, the majority of farmland was devoted to crops. But in the 1880s, railways and steamships made it possible to transport enormous quantities of American and Russian grain to Western Europe. Grain prices fell drastically. To avoid economic disaster, Danish farmers swiftly shifted their emphasis to animal husbandry, particularly dairy and pig farming. Today small farms and agricultural cooperatives efficiently continue this emphasis. Denmark presently has a pig population of more than eight million. In fact, when the British say "Danish," they may be referring to pastry, but more likely they are thinking about bacon. Denmark has been shipping this staple of the British breakfast table across the North Sea for more than a century. In this process they have created powerful shipping companies and become highly skilled in handling perishable foods. With the exception of the Irish Republic, Denmark is the only country in the European Community that is able to export its farm products to the United States, Japan, and other countries with similarly stringent health regulations.

FAMOUS DANES

Hans Christian Andersen (1805–1875) was a famous writer of plays, novels, and travel books. He is best known for his fairy tales, which have been translated into more languages than any other piece of literature except the Bible.

Victor Borge (b. 1909) was a child prodigy who grew up to become a world famous pianist and comedian. The *New York Times* called him the "funniest man who ever lived."

Tycho Brahe (1546–1601), considered the first modern astronomer, discovered the constellation Cassiopeia. His meticulous astronomical observations formed the basis of Johannes Kepler's laws of planetary motion.

Niels Bohr (1885–1932) was a Danish scientist whose theory of the structure of the atom became the basis of quantum physics. He won the Nobel Prize for physics in 1922.

Diderik Buxtehude (1637–1707) was Denmark's first famous composer. As an organist he was so renowned in his day that a young Johann Sebastian Bach traveled more than two hundred miles on foot to hear him play.

Isak Dinesen (1885–1962) was the pen name of Baroness Karen Blixen, a writer who is most famous for her autobiographical novel *Out of Africa* and her Gothic tales.

Søren Kierkegaard (1813–1855), philosopher and theological writer, is known as the father of existentialism.

Carl Nielsen (1865–1931) is Denmark's most famous composer. He wrote symphonies, concertos, chamber music, operas, and choral music. He is considered the father of modern Danish music.

Hans Christian Ørsted (1777–1851) was a scientist who discovered electromagnetism. (A unit of magnetic energy is called an *oersted*.)

Ole Roemer (1644–1710) was an astronomer, physicist, and engineer. He designed the famous waterworks and fountain at Versailles, and he was the first person to measure the speed of light.

Bertal Thorvaldsen (1768–1844) was Denmark's greatest sculptor. He lived in Rome for more than forty years, where he sculpted for princes, kings, and even the Pope.

HIGHLIGHTS OF DANISH HISTORY

810—This year was the death of the first Danish king, **Godfred**, who successfully resisted the northward expansion of the Franks under Charlemagne.

960—This was the year of the baptism of King **Harald Bluetooth** (940–985) who united Denmark and brought Christianity to the Danes.

1013—Harald's son **Sweyn Forkbeard** (d. 1014) conquered England.

1033—By this date the crowns of Denmark, England, and part of Sweden were united under Sweyn's son **Knud the Great** (994–1035). The Danes also controlled Normandy, dominated trade in the Baltic, and wreaked havoc on the Spanish, Italian, and Sicilian coasts.

1397—Norway and Sweden were united under the crown of Denmark as a result of the **Union of Kalmar,** which tried to counter the commercial power of the German-based Hanseatic League.

1471—Sweden chose autonomy; Denmark and Norway were ruled by King **Christian I** (1426–1481).

1536—The civil war ended in Denmark, and the **Danish Lutheran Church** was founded as a result of the Reformation.

1588—**Christian IV** (1577–1648) became king and began a sixty-year reign of prosperity and lasting influence.

1660—**Frederick III** (1609–1670) staged a coup against the nobility and established absolute rule by the Crown.

1814—Denmark was forced to cede Norway to Sweden as a result of her defeat in the Napoleonic Wars.

1849—The Danish constitution was signed, abolishing absolute rule and establishing a government based upon representation. It guaranteed freedom of speech and freedom of religion among other civil liberties. Denmark became the most democratic country in Europe.

1866—Denmark lost the areas of Schleswig and Holstein in southernmost Jutland to Prussia in the Treaty of Prague.

1915—Denmark ratified a new constitution, granting equal voting rights to both men and women.

1933—Denmark gained all of Greenland.

1940—Denmark was invaded and occupied by Nazi Germany.

1949—Denmark joined the North Atlantic Treaty Organization (NATO).

1953—Denmark adopted a new constitution providing for a single-chamber parliament.

1972—Denmark joined the European Economic Community. **Margrethe** (b. 1940), daughter of Frederick IX, became queen of Denmark.

DENMARK'S CHURCHES AND BELLS

In the folktale *A Treasure for Anders,* the villagers needed to build a church. In the century stretching from 1150 to 1250, the Danes built more than two thousand village churches. Many still remain a distinctive and picturesque feature of the Danish landscape. The church was the focal point of community life, so it is not unusual to find Scandinavian legends clustering most thickly around this kind of structure. The church was normally the oldest building in the area, unique in its architecture and contents and intimately connected to the high points of each villager's life.

Bells were also regarded as holy and were believed to be capable of repelling trolls, demons, and thunderstorms. Bells were given names and were even baptized. Entire folktales have arisen concerning bells in which they fly through the air, speak in human voices, and exercise strong wills of their own.

RESOURCES FOR FURTHER STUDY

Thousands of Danish folktales have been collected. Unfortunately, relatively few have been translated into English. Sources of Danish tales that still may be available include *Alexander and the Golden Bird and Other Danish Folk Tales,* translated and retold by Reginald Spink (Edinburgh: Floris Books, 1991); Anna S. Seidelin's *Danish Fairy Tales and Rhymes for Children and Adults*, translated by William V. Zucker (Tucson, Ariz.: Lester Street Publications, 1992); and Svendt Grundtvig's *Danish Fairy Tales*, translated by J. Grant Cramer (New York: Dover, 1972). Danish tales may also be found in collections of Scandinavian folktales. Two collections that should be both accessible and affordable are *Scandinavian Folktales,* collected and translated by Jacqueline Simpson (New York: Penguin Books, 1988); and *Scandinavian Folk and Fairy Tales,* collected from existing English translations by Claire Booss (New York: Crown, 1984). For Danish history, culture, and customs, two Danish Americans (Ingeborg S. MacHaffie and Margaret A. Nielsen) published an informative and very readable book, *On Danish Ways.* Originally published in 1976 by Dillion Press, it was reprinted by Harper and Row in 1992.

A Treasure for Anders

A Folktale from Denmark

Retold by Roger Petersen

Years ago in Denmark, when people still derived their last names from the first name of their father, there lived a farmer named Hans Nielsen (his father's first name had been Niels). Hans lived in the village of Erritsø (uh-RIT-sir) near the town of Fredericia in eastern Jutland. When Hans died, he left his entire estate to his two sons, Henrick and Anders. Hans had divided his money equally between his two sons. Yet because Henrick was the older brother, he received the house, the barn, and two-thirds of his father's livestock and land. It was also his privilege to decide which third would go to his younger brother, Anders.

Henrick decided to give Anders the least productive portion of the land, and he wasted no time in telling his younger brother to build his own house and barn on that poor parcel of ground.

"You may live in my house until you finish building," Henrick said, "but you must pay me rent during that time."

It took almost all of the money that Anders had inherited from his father to build his own house and barn. Anders did all of the work himself, while Henrick lifted not a nail to help him. By the time Anders had finished, he had paid most of his livestock to Henrick for rent. All that Anders took to his new home were a dozen chickens, a few cows, and a horse. He then used the last of his money to buy some simple furniture.

Anders worked very hard. Although he did not have a great deal, he was quite generous with what he owned. No one in need, not even a complete stranger, was turned away hungry or empty-handed from the home of Anders Hansen.

Henrick, on the other hand, was quite unlike his brother. He hoarded his inheritance and kept all his earnings for himself. It was often said in the village that Henrick Hansen could pinch a coin so tightly that the face on the coin would shed tears. Henrick became even richer while Anders remained poor.

10

The village of Erritsø had been in need of a new church for some time now. One day the elders of the village decided to collect money for this project. Despite Henrick's reputation, the elders approached his house with some hope. It was, after all, a worthy undertaking and would benefit so many people.

"You know the poor condition of our church," the elders appealed. "The roof is leaking, the stones are crumbling, and it has hardly enough pews for our parishioners."

Henrick curtly refused to contribute. "I have much better uses for my money than to waste it on some church building. The old one was good enough for my father, and it should be good enough for you! Good day!" Henrick slammed the door in their faces.

The elders walked away and soon arrived at Anders's simple home. They hesitated to ask him for a contribution, for they knew how little Anders had.

"Oh, yes, the village definitely needs a new church," agreed Anders as he opened a small metal box. "Unfortunately, it seems that my contribution may only be enough to purchase two hymnals." Anders emptied the box of its few coins and handed them to the elders. "Please take these. I am sorry that there is not more." Only after much insistence did the elders take the last of Anders' money. He had the desire, but not the means. His brother Henrick had the means, but no desire.

Anders went to bed that night sorrowful that he was unable to give more to the new church. He remembered what his father used to say: "It is no disgrace to be poor, but it can be inconvenient."

"If I had the money, I'd build the entire church," Anders resolved as he fell asleep.

Later that night Anders heard a voice saying, "Go to the bridge at Sønder (SERN-der) and you will discover a treasure."

Anders awakened. "Is someone there?" he called out. There was no reply. He lit a candle. No one was in the room. "Perhaps it was the sound of the wind," Anders thought. He lay back down and soon fell asleep.

Sometime later Anders again heard someone say, "Go to the bridge at Sønder and you will discover a treasure." Anders sat up in bed. "Who is there?" Again there was no answer. There was no sound, not even the sound of the wind. Anders lit the candle and looked all over the house. He found no one. "I must have been dreaming," Anders reasoned. For the third time that night Anders went to bed, but he left the candle lit this time.

He had been sleeping for only an hour when he again heard a voice saying, "Go to the bridge at Sønder and you will discover a treasure." Anders again sat up in bed. The candle was still lit and the room was still empty.

"Very well," Anders cried out, "I will go to the bridge at Sønder tomorrow if only I can get some sleep tonight!" Anders lay back down and slept peacefully until dawn.

After eating breakfast and packing some bread and cheese for lunch, Anders set off. He walked the ten miles to the bridge at Sønder, which is near the town of Vejle (VIH-lah).

Anders arrived at the bridge and waited, and waited, and waited. He did not even know what he was waiting for; he was simply obeying the voice in his dream. Anders walked back and forth across the bridge. He walked under the bridge. He walked beyond the bridge and looked back. At no time did he see any treasure.

"Perhaps there is a message written on the bridge," thought Anders. He examined the bridge for markings. But there were no markings, no messages, no clues. Any hope he had was dimming with the setting sun.

Anders decided to return home. As he turned to leave, an officer of the army approached him. "I noticed that you spent all day at this bridge," the officer began. "Are you waiting for someone?"

"I am waiting for a treasure," Anders explained. "Last night I had the same dream three times. In the dream a voice told me that if I went to the bridge at Sønder, I would discover a treasure. But I have been here all day and have discovered nothing."

"Perhaps you have discovered that you cannot put any stock in dreams," the officer laughed. "Last night I too had a dream. In my dream a voice told me that if I went to Erritsø and dug in the northwest corner of a barn owned by an Anders Hansen, I

would find a treasure. And I am certainly not going to waste my time going there."

Without saying any more than goodbye, Anders ran home, grabbed a shovel, and began to dig in the northwest corner of his barn. It was not long before Anders uncovered an ancient chest. From its markings, it appeared to be a Viking chest. It was filled with gold and silver coins.

"There is certainly enough money here to build a church!" Anders exclaimed. "Tomorrow we will pick the site." The next morning Anders gathered the town elders and related all that had happened. He urged them to decide upon a site for the church that very day. His enthusiasm was contagious and the elders readily agreed. They all marched off to look for a site. As Anders and the elders were surveying a particular field, Henrick happened to ride by.

"Anders! What are you doing?"

"I am going to build a church for the parish, and we are trying to decide on the best site for it."

"Oh, really?" Henrick snickered. "If *you* ever build a church, then *I* will supply the bells for it." Henrick rode off laughing scornfully.

But Anders did build the church, thus compelling Henrick to spend a great sum of money for its bells. All of this took its toll on Henrick, and he died shortly afterward. Folks say he died of grief. Was it because he had to spend so much money on bells, or was it because the land on which the enormous treasure was found could have been his?

Source: The motif involving the manner in which Anders discovered the treasure occurs in the folklore of Denmark and many other cultures. One version is found in J. M. Thiele's collection, *Danmarks Folkesagen,* (Volume 1, pp. 246–247), published in Copenhagen in 1843, with the title "The Church at Erritsø."

A Treasure for Anders (Denmark)— Follow-Up Information and Activities

WHAT'S IN A NAME?

The practice of deriving one's last name from the first name of the father dates back to the ancient Vikings, who lived in small, limited societies. They used this method to distinguish among family clans. Thus Anders's last name was Hansen because his father's first name was Hans (*sen* indicates "son" in Danish). If Anders had a son and named him Peter, his name would have been Peter Andersen. If Anders had a daughter and named her Kristen, she would have been Kristen Anderdatter (*datter* is the Danish word for "daughter"). As the Danish population grew, this practice caused tremendous confusion, although it continued until 1828 when the Danish government passed the Name Law requiring all families to choose a permanent surname for the future. Any Scandinavian or Anglo-Saxon name ending in -*sen* or -*son* originated in the Norse patronymic system.

The most common Danish name is Jensen (7.7% of the population). Almost as common are the names Nielsen (7.3%) and Hansen (6.2%), followed closely by a host of Christensens, Andersens, Petersens, and Pedersens. In fact, two-thirds of all Danish names end in -*sen*.

Let's take another look at Anders's family:

Father:
Hans Nielsen
↓
Sons:
Henrick Hansen and Anders Hansen

Henrick's son: Knud Henricksen   **Anders's son**: Bjorn Andersen
Henrick's daughter: Martha Henrickdatter   **Anders's daughter**: Lisa Anderdatter

If **Bjorn Andersen** had had both a son and a daughter, write a possible name for each of them:

_____

If YOU had been born in Denmark before 1828, your name would have been different. Fill in the name possibilities in the following blank spaces:

Your father's name: _____

What your name would have been: _____

Possible name for your son or daughter (or both): _____

It gets complicated, doesn't it? It is easy to see why the Danish passed the Name Law. Denmark wasn't the only country with names generated in this fashion, however. Investigate the history of this procedure in other cultures to determine if this same practice occurred. What about the names O'Dell or MacDonald, for example? All names have a history. Look at the names of the people in your classroom. Do you think any of them have an origin similar to the Danish practice described here? How many of the last names of your classmates refer to occupations? What other interesting last names can you find?

A Treasure for Anders (Denmark)— Follow-Up Information and Activities

DANISH PROVERBS

"It is no disgrace to be poor, but it is inconvenient."

In *A Treasure for Anders,* Anders remembered this proverb when he wanted to give money to build the church. Many proverbs reflect a major consideration regarding a struggle in someone's life. Consider some additional Danish proverbs:

The miser's bag is never full.
The nobler the blood, the less the pride.
Better to ask twice than to lose your way.
The fall of a leaf is a whisper to the living.
There is no cure against a slanderer's bite.
Don't sail out farther than you can row back.
They are cheated most who cheat themselves.
Care and not fine stables makes a good horse.
An old error has more friends than a new truth.
He who is afraid of asking is ashamed of learning.
Fools are like other folks as long as they are silent.
Flattery is sweet food for those who can swallow it.
It is better to suffer for truth than to prosper by falsehood.
The person who loves sorrow will always find something to mourn about.

After thinking about these proverbs, select one or more of the following exercises, and write your answers on separate paper.

Exercise 1. Anders recalled a proverb that he remembered his father saying. Discuss the meaning of that proverb as it relates to this story. Do you agree with its premise?

Exercise 2. Select one of the proverbs in the list provided here and relate it to either Anders or Henrick. *Example:* Henrick was disappointed when he discovered he had given away land that contained a hidden treasure. Yet had he found it, he would still have been unhappy, because a "miser's bag is never full."

Exercise 3. What other proverbs have you heard? Select one proverb and use it in a brief story. *Example:* "A stitch in time saves nine." My younger brother had a small rip in his jacket sleeve. He kept on wearing it until the entire sleeve came loose from his jacket. It took Mom more than an hour to sew it back together, but she could have mended it earlier in just a few minutes. After all, a stitch in time saves nine.

A Treasure for Anders (Denmark)—
Follow-Up Information and Activities

THE DANISH LANGUAGE

The majority of all languages spoken today were formed from earlier languages. For example, the English language you speak was primarily formed from Latin and Greek. Many of our words are influenced by a variety of other customs and cultures, however. Column A below includes Danish words. You may be able to determine what they mean because of the similarity of their spellings to English words with close meanings. Write their matching letter by the English words. Be careful—some are tricky!

Column A: Danish Words

A. advokat

B. apotek

C. butterfly

D. chef

E. cirka

F. cowboybukser

G. cykel

H. fabrik

I. handske

J. hoppe

K. kasse

L. kaste

M. slippe

N. salat

O. sky

P. slagter

Column B: English Words

_____ 1. bow tie

_____ 2. jeans

_____ 3. box

_____ 4. factory

_____ 5. glove

_____ 6. pharmacy

_____ 7. throw

_____ 8. cloud

_____ 9. butcher

_____ 10. lettuce

_____ 11. cut

_____ 12. lawyer

_____ 13. boss

_____ 14. bicycle

_____ 15. jump

_____ 16. lemon

Answers: A-12, B-6, C-1, D-13, E-16, F-2, G-14, H-4, I-5, J-15, K-3, L-7, M-11, N-10, O-8, P-9.

A Treasure for Anders (Denmark)— Follow-Up Information and Activities

INVESTIGATION CARDS FOR
A TREASURE FOR ANDERS

Investigation Card 1: Dream On
"A Treasure for Anders"

The dream Anders had in this story resulted in a major change in his life. Do you believe your dreams carry messages that you should heed? What information can you find about the meaning of dreams? Investigate this area until you have found three items of information that you would consider to be facts. Now find three beliefs or suppositions about dreams that you would consider to be someone's opinion rather than actual facts.

Investigation Card 2: The Bell Sell
"A Treasure for Anders"

Henrick became very depressed because he had to pay for the bells for the new church. Investigate the possible costs of bells (either current costs or costs during earlier times in Denmark). What percentage of the total cost of a church might the bell costs have been then or might be today?

Investigation Card 3: Here and There
"A Treasure for Anders"

Read the page entitled "Facts About Denmark." Select one of these facts (or a group of facts) and contrast these facts with those of the country in which you live.

Investigation Card 4: Danish Symbols
"A Treasure for Anders"

Two words in this story contain a symbol that is not used to spell English words. This symbol is ø. What sound does this symbol generally represent in Danish? Can you find other Danish words that contain this symbol? What symbols in other languages can you find that do not exist in English? Make a list of these symbols, followed by examples of words containing them.

A Treasure for Anders (Denmark)—
Follow-Up Information and Activities

DRAMA ACTIVITY CARDS FOR
A TREASURE FOR ANDERS

Drama Activity Card 1: Adventure in Time
"A Treasure for Anders"
Two Characters Needed: You and Henrick

You have just stepped into a time machine and will shortly be taken back to the setting of this story. You want to interview Henrick for a major television network. Enact this interview.

Drama Activity Card 2: Bridging the Gap
"A Treasure for Anders"
Two Characters Needed: Anders and an Army Officer

Anders later decided to go back to the same bridge at Sønder. The same army officer was nearby. Enact a conversation the two might have had.

Drama Activity Card 3: Sweet Dreams
"A Treasure for Anders"
Two Characters Needed: Anders and a Friend

After hearing about Anders' dream, one of his friends decided to play a trick on him. The friend hid in Anders' bedroom and waited until Anders was asleep. The friend then pretended to be the voice in a dream. Enact such a scene.

Drama Activity Card 4: My Daddy is Better Than Yours
"A Treasure for Anders"
Two (or more) Characters Needed: Children of Anders and Henrick

Years after this story was over, the children of Anders and Henrick were playing together. They were trying to recall the story about the building of the church and the purchase of the bells. Each child is filled with bias for his/her own father. Enact this conversation.

A Treasure for Anders (Denmark)—
Follow-Up Information and Activities

CREATIVE WRITING CARDS FOR
A TREASURE FOR ANDERS

Creative Writing Card 1: The Bell Bill
"A Treasure for Anders"

Pretend you were the official treasurer for the village of Erritsø.
You have been asked to present Henrick with the bill for the
church bells. You are afraid to approach him directly, so you have
decided to prepare a statement showing what he owes. Design such a bill.

Creative Writing Card 2: The Eulogy
"A Treasure for Anders"

The elders of the village of Erritsø asked Anders to deliver a eulogy
at Henrick's funeral. (A eulogy is a speech of high praise.
Eulogies are often given at funerals.) Anders reflected on
the treatment he had received from Henrick, and he thought
about the reputation of his brother in the village.
Keeping in the character of Anders, write a possible eulogy
he might have delivered at his brother's funeral.

Creative Writing Card 3: Take a Letter
"A Treasure for Anders"

You are a village leader in Erritsø. You were in the group that requested funding
for the church from Henrick. You feel that you were treated rudely when
making this request. Write a letter to Henrick to inform him of the
feelings of the villagers regarding his reactions to this request.

Creative Writing Card 4: The Dream
"A Treasure for Anders"

After reading this story, you have an unusual dream.
Write a story in which your dream is a major part of the plot.

A Treasure for Anders (Denmark)— Wrap-Up Activity

GAME SHOW FUN

To leaders of the game show activities: Use the following questions in your favorite game show format. (See page xv for activity suggestions.) These questions may be shown on an overhead projector or prepared as separate cards. For an easier round of questions, include the four choices of answers. For a more challenging experience, use only the question stem (without the choices of answers). The questions relate to the story content only. (Answers appear on page xvi.) Additional questions may be prepared from the specific cultural information provided in this section or discovered by the involved learners.

Questions from the Story Content

1. How did Hans (the father) divide his money, livestock, and land between his two sons?

    A. Henrick and Anders each received exactly half of everything.

    B. Anders received two-thirds of everything, but they were the least desired parts.

    C. Henrick received half the money and two-thirds of the livestock and land.

    D. Henrick inherited everything, but he gave a small portion to Anders.

2. What one factor caused the difference in the inheritance amounts?

    A. Age

    B. Height

    C. Intelligence

    D. Attitude

3. What did Anders do with most of the livestock that he inherited?

    A. He gave it to neighbors in need.

    B. Most of it wandered away and died.

    C. He sold it to get enough money to build the new church.

    D. He gave it to Henrick for rent.

4. Why was the town of Erritsø building a new church?

    A. Arsonists had burned the old one.

    B. The existing church was too small and in a state of disrepair.

    C. The church was on land needed by the government.

    D. The current church was on Henrick's land, and he wouldn't allow the villagers to worship without paying rent.

5. What was Henrick's response when he was asked to donate money to build the new church?

    A. He was rude to the solicitors, and he gave them nothing.

    B. He told them he would think about it, and he asked them to return later.

    C. He offered to give a large sum if they would name the church after him.

    D. He told them to get the money from his brother instead of bothering him with such a silly request.

6. Describe the amount of the first contribution Anders made to the new church.

    A. It was enough to buy two hymnals.

    B. It paid for the bells.

    C. It paid for everything except the bells.

    D. He gave no money at all, but he gave many hours of his time to help build the church.

7. Both Anders and an officer had a dream about a treasure. What was the difference in how they responded to their dreams?

    A. Neither thought his own dream was worth pursuing.

    B. Both were anxious to find the treasure mentioned in the dream.

    C. Anders was puzzled but pursued it; the officer laughed at the idea.

    D. Anders followed the instructions immediately; the officer waited several days.

8. How did Anders learn the details about where the treasure could be found?

   A. It was written on the side of the bridge in Sønder.

   B. He overheard some fishermen talk about where the treasure was located.

   C. A church elder gave him the instructions.

   D. The location was revealed through someone else's dream.

9. What was the physical location of the treasure?

   A. It was hidden inside a chest in the basement of the old church.

   B. It was buried near a corner of his own barn.

   C. It was beneath a Viking bridge in Sønder.

   D. It was sitting just across the border on Henrick's property.

10. Why did Henrick offer to buy the bells for the new church?

   A. He hoped that when the church bells rang, all of the villagers would be reminded of his generous contribution.

   B. He wanted to "one-up" his brother.

   C. He sarcastically offered to do so when he heard that Anders planned to build the church.

   D. He was a very religious man, and this was just one way to prove his faith.

11. What did the author imply was the cause of Henrick's death?

   A. His greed may have overwhelmed him.

   B. He died of overexertion from transporting the heavy church bells.

   C. After digging up the treasure, he fell dead.

   D. He died of old age.

Questions About Denmark and Its Culture

12. Why did churches play a significant role in the early Danish cultures?

    A. They were the focal point of community life and were often the basis of legends and folklore.

    B. They were relatively scarce because the villagers rarely attended the services.

    C. The buildings were used for worship services but their use primarily centered around schools and commerce.

    D. Only the wealthy were allowed to participate in the churches' worship activities.

13. What reputation did church bells have in early Danish cultures?

    A. Church bells were a sign of great wealth, and the extremely wealthy even had bell towers built in their homes.

    B. Church bells were so revered that only the dignitaries could actually ring them.

    C. The sound of the church bells were believed to transmit messages to people while they were sleeping.

    D. Church bells were thought to be holy and capable of repelling trolls, demons, and thunderstorms.

14. Who is the famous writer from Denmark widely known for his fairy tales?

    A. Christopher Henricksen

    B. Victor Borge

    C. Hans Christian Andersen

    D. Carl Anders Nielsen

15. Today, more than two-thirds of Denmark's land is used for what purpose?

    A. Industry

    B. Farming

    C. Churches

    D. Raising pigs

Chapter 2

The Three Reeds

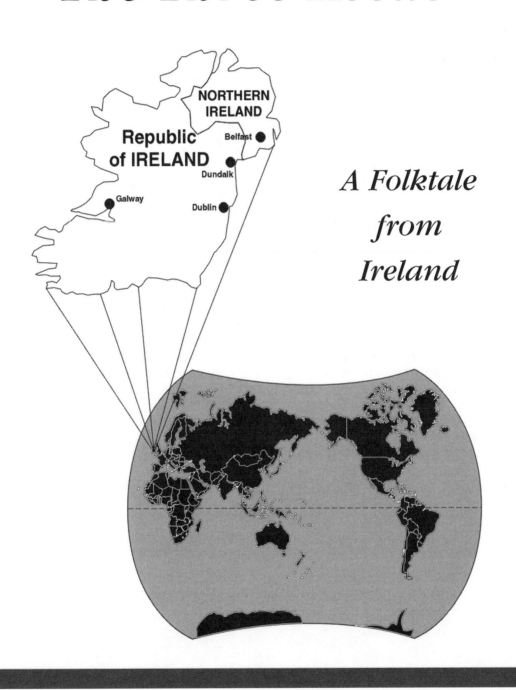

A Folktale

from

Ireland

About the Contributor

This section was prepared primarily by

Maggi Kerr Peirce

Maggi Kerr Peirce (pronounced *purse*) was born in Belfast, Northern Ireland, and has lived in the United States since 1964. Residing all of her childhood in the city of Belfast, she grew up surrounded by songs, skipping rhymes, and recitations in front of the "grown-ups" on all festive occasions. She has taught classes in storytelling and was artist-in-residence in Bonner County, Idaho, in 1986. She recently performed in *The Irish Writers' Series* in Boston, and she represented Northern Ireland at the Smithsonian's *Campus on the Mall.* She is currently a writer and performer with numerous impressive accomplishments, publications, and honors relating to the Irish culture.

In 2001, Maggi was the recipient of the Oracle Lifetime Achievement Award from the National Storytelling Network for her "sustained and exemplary contributions to storytelling."

The Three Reeds (Ireland)— Cultural Background

STORY INFORMATION

When the English crushed the Irish rebellion of 1641–1642, a law was passed that made it a crime to educate anyone in Ireland who did not belong to the established church. This forced the Irish to rely on more ancient methods, such as storytelling, to pass on their culture and beliefs from one generation to the next; and they were quite accomplished at this form of communication. *The Three Reeds* is an example of such a story.

Folktales told in different cultures frequently have words that might be unfamiliar. Some words in this story are explained here.

Road men are laborers who repaired holes in the road.

Tea refers to supper in the British Commonwealth. "Morning tea" and "afternoon tea" are snack times. An optional activity for listeners prior to hearing this story would be to list words in their own culture that pertain to daily meals and snacks.

Haverin' is a derogatory term that describes the chatter of the old man in the story. It is similar to the English term *babble*.

Da is a short version of "Dad."

Even the word **Ireland** has an interesting background. Learners could explore other names for Ireland and investigate their origins and meanings. (Some examples are Hibernia, Eire, Emerald Isle, and Erin.) The proximity of Dundalk to the border between the two Irelands—Eire and Northern Ireland—sets this story into the role of an allegory for that divided country. Before listening to or reading the story, learners could investigate when the two countries separated. Dundalk was captured in 1315 by Edward Bruce, who later (1318) was defeated near there by the army of Edward II. Learners could investigate the background of Edward Bruce, who proclaimed himself king.

Listeners may also want to discuss a crop associated with Ireland: potatoes. The causes and results of several devastating potato famines in the 1800s could be explored. The massive immigration to North and South America to escape the famines introduced Irish culture to many parts of the world. Learners could volunteer any information they already have regarding Irish customs or practices.

The Three Reeds

A Folktale from Ireland

Retold by Maggi Kerr Peirce

Families quarrel. They do, and they can't help it. Some brothers and sisters get along famously, and others are at one another's throats from the day they come into this world. This story is about the fear an old man had that his sons would quarrel when he was no longer on this earth. Many people in American cultures don't like to discuss death, but in Ireland it is as much a part of living as birth. The old man in this story, who lived south of Dundalk (the capital of County Louth), instinctively knew that his days were numbered.

Once an old man had three sons named William, James, and John. They were good, dutiful sons. That wasn't easy, mind you, because their mother had died when Johnny, the youngest, was five or six years old. When the father became too weak to care for himself, they had kindly brought him down to the heart of the house. That was the kitchen, of course, and they'd set up a cozy bed in the corner where he could watch the road for a bit o' life. He could also talk with whoever came in, maybe Mary-Ellen who brought fresh eggs from down the road or one of the road men coming in for water.

For many's the long day this arrangement pleased the old man well, but finally he felt the wing of death stroke him gently as he lay in the afternoon sunlight. As soon as William returned from work, his father called out to him.

"What is it you want, father?" William turned round to hang his cap on the hook, and the old man answered.

"I want you to go to the river and pick me the two best reeds that you can find and bring them here to me."

William—slow, dependable, and plodding—stuck his cap back on his head and made for the road through the stockyard.

James strode into the kitchen, and the father gave him the same order, "James, go and fetch me the two strongest reeds you can find in the river."

Now James was not as compliant as William. He was hungry, and he needed his tea. Out he went muttering under his breath, just in time to bump into William who held in his hands two strong reeds, each streaming with water.

James met Johnny on the doorstep. "The ol' man's haverin'," he said, and he stomped off toward the river. But when young Johnny heard the request that his father made, he eagerly said, "Fine, Da, I'll pick the best," and he hurried off wondering with excitement what it all meant. When you live in a lonely place, anything even a bit surprising can lift your mind from the humdrum.

After all three had returned, the old man surveyed his three fine sons in front of him. Each held two reeds that had been pulled from the river. The father struggled to sit up, and Johnny plumped up the two pillows behind him.

"Give me the best reed of the two," the father said to each of his sons. Carefully William, James, and John examined their two reeds, and William then handed their father his choice. The sick man rose, and with a deft flick of his fingers he split the reed in half. He held out his hand, ready for James's reed. That reed, too, was snapped in half and thrown to the floor.

"Well," he said, "Johnny lad, is yours any better?" Quickly his youngest son handed over a sturdy strong reed, looking triumphantly at his older brothers.

"Snap!" the sound crackled in the air.

The old man leaned forward slowly. "Boys," he said, "come closer and give me your remaining reeds."

Three pairs of eyes were fastened on him. Breathing with difficulty, the father painstakingly braided (or plaited) the three reeds as if they were someone's long hair.

"Now try to break this, William," he said. A sly smile crept along the corner of his mouth.

William struggled, but was unable to break the braided reeds.

"Now you, James."

James, too, was unsuccessful.

"Now you, Johnny lad."

Each of his sons pulled and pushed until they were red in the face, but it was no use. Their father smiled up at them and said, "Now, lads, I have shown you this day that only in unity is there strength. Long after I am dead and gone, remember the lesson you have learned this day." Then he closed his eyes and slept peacefully that night.

And when his time did come—as Death does to us all—his good, dutiful sons, all different in their ways and manners, remembered what their old father had taught them. There was never an ill word among them, and they lived in peace and contentment to the end of their days.

The Three Reeds (Ireland)—
Follow-Up Information and Activities

ABOUT IRISH FOLKTALES

Did you notice that the old man in this folktale was not given a name? In some older folktales, names were often not given to the main characters. These tales were usually about ordinary *folks*—not princes, kings, or wild warriors whose names should be remembered. When there were three sons in a tale that originated in Ireland, however, typical names included William, James, and John. If you were writing a folktale reflecting aspects of your own culture, would you give the father a name? If so, what name would you choose?

_____

What names would you choose for the three sons? _____

Did you notice the number three in this tale? (There were three sons and two times three reeds.) The number three is a magic number in Ireland. In many Irish folktales there are three questions, three tasks, or three riddles that have to be dealt with. In the daily routine in Ireland, if two accidents happen, folks always wait for the third . . . and it invariably comes. When it does, they say, "Thank god, there's the third," and they know that the ill luck has passed. They also use the phrase "Third time lucky." Does the phrase "Third time lucky" have a counterpart in your culture? If so, how is it stated?

_____

_____

In the folktales of your culture, is there a magic number that might be used in the plot? If so, what is it?

_____

Make a list of some other expressions in your culture that contain numerals.

_____

_____

There are different types of folktales. Think about what type of folktale *The Three Reeds* might be. The author classifies it as a "moralistic" folktale—one that teaches readers or listeners a good lesson because of the moral either stated or implied. Another type of story that also has a moral is the fable. Fables have animals as their main characters, and they usually end with a statement that summarizes the lesson to be learned. State the lesson that could be learned from *The Three Reeds:*

_____

_____

_____

The Three Reeds (Ireland)—
Follow-Up Information and Activities

IRISH HOMES AND CARE FOR THE ELDERLY

Folktales sometimes provide information about many aspects of other cultures, such as how people built their homes and what functions occurred in different rooms. Heating methods are sometimes reflected through the details of a folktale. Even today few British or Irish homes have central heating. Rural homes in Ireland often use **peat** for heating. Find out what peat is and how it is obtained.

_____

_____

_____

Investigate the manner in which Irish farmhouses were constructed in the 1800s. Many had roofs made of sod (soil and live grass). What advantage would such a roof provide?

_____

_____

_____

In the folktale *The Three Reeds,* the sons moved their father into the kitchen after he became unable to care for himself. Why do you think they chose the kitchen instead of a bedroom or other room in their house?

_____

_____

_____

If you had an elderly person living at your house, would he or she live in the kitchen? Why or why not?

_____

_____

_____

Why didn't the sons place their father in a nursing home?

_____

_____

When a parent or grandparent in your culture becomes too old to care for himself or herself, what are the most common choices for such care?

_____

_____

The Three Reeds (Ireland)—
Follow-Up Information and Activities

FARMING IN IRELAND

The setting of this story was the east coast of Ireland. This part of Ireland has rich and fertile land. Western Ireland, however, has land that is essentially useless for farming. How does the land in this story contrast with the land in your area regarding its usefulness for farming?

_____

_____

_____

_____

The farm in this story contained only about five acres. The family needed to plant enough crops on these five acres to provide the majority of their annual food and clothing needs. Tell what you think they might have planted on such a small piece of ground.

_____

Why were all three sons in this story still unmarried, at ages when young men in other agricultural societies would already be rearing families? Why were they still living at home? Investigate how the scarcity of available farmland after the Great Famine of 1845–1847 was responsible for changes in many of the social customs in Ireland (such as marriage), as well as a determining factor in choosing a career or vocation.

_____

_____

_____

What is the closest farm near you? Contrast that farm with the one in this story. Could the farm near you produce enough crops to keep a family alive for a year? Tell why or why not.

_____

_____

_____

Are there individuals in your state who earn their living by farming? If so, what crops do they produce? Is it necessary for them to feed their families with their own produce? Find out at least five interesting facts about farming in your region or state.

_____

_____

_____

The Three Reeds (Ireland)—
Follow-Up Information and Activities

A LESSON FROM IRELAND

Consider what has happened in Ireland during the past two or three decades regarding the ability of the people to work together in unity. Do you think the people in Ireland should tell this folktale to their families and communities? Are there other communities that could profit from the lesson in *The Three Reeds*? Are there groups in your own school or community who should hear this story? Select one group that you think could profit most from thinking about the lesson in this folktale. Tell why you selected that group and what the outcome might be if they thought seriously about this lesson.

_____

_____

_____

_____

_____

_____

_____

_____

_____

_____

_____

_____

_____

_____

_____

_____

_____

_____

_____

_____

_____

The Three Reeds (Ireland)—
Wrap-Up Activity

GAME SHOW FUN

To leaders of the game show activities: Use the following questions in your favorite game show format. (See page xv for activity suggestions.) These questions may be shown on an overhead projector or prepared as separate cards. For an easier round of questions, include the four choices of answers. For a more challenging experience, use only the question stem (without the choices of answers). The questions relate to the story content only. (Answers appear on page xvi.) Additional questions may be prepared from the specific cultural information provided in this section or discovered by the involved learners.

Questions from the Story Content

1. Which character in this story would likely be voted the family's "most eager and cooperative"?

   A. The first son (William)

   B. The second son (James)

   C. The third son (Johnny)

   D. The father

2. Why was the kitchen selected as the place to put the old man's bed?

   A. The old man needed frequent meals because of his illness, and having his bed in the kitchen saved many steps for the sons during mealtimes.

   B. It was the heart of the house. From there the old man could observe the most action and initiate the most conversations.

   C. The old man was training his sons in meal preparation, and by having his bed in the kitchen he could more easily give instructions.

   D. The humidity from the foods that were cooking greatly assisted in the old man's dehydration problems.

3. What two items from the story illustrate the significance of the numeral three?

   A. The three sons wore three braids in their hair.

   B. The father gave three wishes to each of the three sons.

   C. Three generations of men made three trips to the river.

   D. There were three sons and three reeds in the braid.

4. Why did the father break one of the reeds each son had brought him?

   A. To complete the first step of the lesson he was trying to teach them

   B. To demonstrate his physical strength to his sons

   C. To have six equal-size pieces for the braid he wanted to make

   D. To create a task for his sons that would prove which one was worthy to inherit his wealth

5. Without the father's reed-breaking demonstration, how might the three sons have dealt with a major decision in their future?

   A. They might have broken more than three reeds each time they made a major decision.

   B. They would have quarreled among themselves rather than working together.

   C. They might have moved away from the river.

   D. They might have consulted with neighbors before making an important decision.

Questions About Vocabulary Terms from the Story

6. In most English cultures, instead of saying that an old person was "haverin'," what word might be used?

   A. Babbling

   B. Lying

   C. Hollering

   D. Screaming

7. The old man asked each of his sons to bring back two reeds from the river. In this case, what is a reed?

   A. A wind instrument made from the hollow joint of a plant

   B. A type of tall grass with a slender stem

   C. A device on a loom resembling a comb

   D. A vegetable that grows in damp soil and adds a spicy flavor to foods

8. Of the words *complaining, compliant, complimentary,* and *compassionate,* which best describes the first son?

   A. Complaining

   B. Compliant

   C. Complimentary

   D. Compassionate

9. In this story "road men" came into the house for water. What was the job of these road men?

   A. They drove to each home in the village to deliver essential supplies.

   B. They served as lawmen to deter robberies and other criminal acts.

   C. They repaired holes in the road.

   D. They were popular entertainers in traveling road shows.

10. What is another word used in this story to mean *braid*?

   A. Brat

   B. Bread

   C. Plate

   D. Plait

Questions About Ireland and Its Culture—
From the Provided Information and from Outside Sources

11. After the Irish rebellion of 1641–1642 was crushed, what was a major reason many Irish families shared stories (such as this folktale) with each other?

   A. To pass on their culture and beliefs from one generation to the next (because they were barred from receiving a formal education)

   B. For evening entertainment (because there were no televisions or theaters)

   C. To develop their communication and oral performance skills

   D. To help the young ones calm down enough so they would easily drift off to sleep at bedtime

12. Most American cultures refer to the three daily meals as breakfast, lunch, and dinner. What would be a comparable word for "dinner" in Ireland?

   A. Supper

   B. Brunch

   C. Break time

   D. Tea

13. In the 1800s Ireland's major crop failed, resulting in famine. What was the crop?

   A. Tomatoes

   B. Potatoes

   C. Wheat

   D. Soybeans

14. How did this famine affect people living in Ireland at that time?

   A. Neighboring countries were able to import about 80,000 tons of food—enough to keep the majority of the people from starving.

   B. Before many people starved to death, farmers substituted other crops in time to save them.

   C. About 750,000 people died of starvation or disease, and several hundred thousand escaped to other parts of the world.

   D. Miraculously, only a few died because of the skilled planning of the government officials.

15. What is both the capital of Ireland and its largest city?

   A. Emerald Isle

   B. Galway

   C. Donegal

   D. Dublin

Chapter 3

The Lorelei

A Folktale

from

Germany

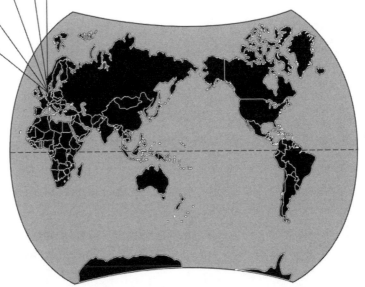

About the Contributor

This section was prepared primarily by

Wendy Welch

Wendy Welch holds a bachelor of science degree in German and journalism and a master's degree in story arts. She moved to Bonn, Germany, in 1992 and studied German history at Friedrich-Wilhelms Universität. Traveling throughout Germany often took her along the Rhine, which fueled her fascination with the river and its history. She also regularly visited the Köln Cathedral, located about twenty minutes from her apartment in Bonn. Wendy visited twenty-eight countries in Europe and Asia and took advantage of the opportunity to collect stories. As a member of a touring arts team based in Los Angeles, she performed in most of those countries. Her experiences in such culturally diverse locations are reflected in the stories on her audiotape, *Story Sampler.* She won the Tennessee Press Association's Reporting Award in 1993 and has since engaged in a variety of storytelling performances and graduate studies.

The Lorelei (Germany)— Cultural Background

The information that follows will assist in understanding the cultural background for the story *The Lorelei*.

STORY LOCALE: THE RHINE

The Rhine (*Der Rhein* in German) is the mostly peaceful river down which Dieter and his father ferry their load of coal in *The Lorelei*. Scattered along its banks are abandoned castles, reminders of the Rhine's strategic importance in the olden days. Besides playing a crucial role in the economic development of Germany, the Rhine is the center of many additional stories. Some of these have to do with the hazards of river life. Although the Rhine was important for transporting goods across Europe, it was very dangerous. Boats in the Middle Ages were not as well built as they are now; they often capsized and their passengers drowned. Pirates stood along the cliffs lining the rivers and ordered the boatmen to give up all their valuables. If the boatmen refused, the pirates would sink their crafts by throwing rocks down from the cliffs.

STORY SETTING: THE CRUSADES

In the story *The Lorelei*, Günther is on his way to fight in the Third Crusade. The Crusades (1095–1270) were part of a prominent period in the development of Western Europe. Many interesting books have been written about that time, including ***Robin Hood, Ivanhoe,*** and ***The Door in the Wall.*** You might enjoy reading one of these books, and you might check your library under "Crusades," "Chivalry," or "Middle Ages" for other books about this era.

During the Crusades, it was sometimes difficult to follow who was fighting whom for what. Although they began as a series of Holy Wars to free Jerusalem from the Turks, by the Fourth Crusade in 1203, the crusaders were attacking not the Turks, but the people of Constantinople, the capital city of Byzantium, the empire they were supposed to be helping! In later crusades, the German emperor made treaties with the Turks against the Byzantines. Further reading about the Crusades can offer insight into the saying, "Politics makes strange bedfellows."

BACKGROUND: WOMEN AND ROMANCE

European women in the cultures of the Middle Ages did not have many rights, but they did have some influence. Although they gave up whatever property they might possess to their husbands when they married, they were mistresses of the household, in charge of maintaining it, and those fortunate enough to live in castles were largely responsible for building the romantic stereotype of the knight still popular today. Ladies in the Age of Chivalry founded the idea of romantic love so prevalent through the fifteenth century.

Even though they controlled the popular theories of romance, women had little control over whom they would marry. Lorelei wanted to marry someone who would love her for herself, not for her beauty. This characteristic, however, was atypical of the culture at that time. Most women accepted their romantic fate without exercising the bravery demonstrated by Lorelei.

The Lorelei

A Folktale from Germany

Retold by Wendy Welch

Dieter and his father floated their coal-laden barge down the Rhine River.[1] It was a beautiful day, thirteen-year-old Dieter noted with pleasure. Sunlight skimmed the water's rippled surface, the cliffs gleamed in the light, and the calls of birds added a pleasant melody to the whispering of tiny waves against the rocky banks. But even as the peaceful scene lulled Dieter into relaxing his downstream watch, his father called sharply, "Achtung! ["attention!"; ak-TOONG] We're coming to Loreleiberg [LORE-uh-LIE-burg]!"

Although his body was covered in sweat from the heat, Dieter shivered as he leapt to help his father maneuver the treacherous bend in the river just before the cliff. The sharp curve seemed to appear from nowhere. The river narrowed at the bend, the currents became fierce, and the huge rock known as Loreleiberg jutted out over the water just beyond. Dieter looked down to see his oar disappear in the blackness of the water below, shivering again as he thought of the seemingly bottomless depths beneath him.

They negotiated the turn with little trouble. Dieter's father was a skilled ferryman, and he had taught his son well—everything from how to turn his oar to why he should never look up at Loreleiberg, under whose shadow they now passed.

Dieter was eleven when he first heard "The Lorelei" (LORE-uh-LIE). It was a wonderful memory because his father, Dieter's favorite storyteller, had told it on their first trip together down the Rhine. He remembered how his father had looked, pulling on his oar, one eye on the river, while telling the tragic tale. So long ago it had happened—in the 1100s. Dieter could hardly fathom such a far-off time. Here is how the tale was told.

Lorelei was a beautiful and kindhearted woman, although some people enviously called her cruel and heartless because of the number of suitors she turned away. Blue eyes like twinkling stars, hair as bright as summer sun shining on fields of wheat—her loveliness made her not only the target of petty jealousy, but also the object of unwanted attention from an endless string of knights and barons asking for her hand in marriage. Her attitude toward them was always the same: pity that her beauty caused them such pain as she turned them all away. In fact, some said Lorelei considered her beauty a curse. When she attended tournaments, fights broke out among the knights as to who would crown her queen of the festivities.[2] This grieved Lorelei, for her secret desire was to marry someone whose affection for her would not fade with her beauty as she grew older. She never found him in the stream of young men who came to woo her.

She found him in Günther, a wandering knight on his way to the Crusades to join Frederick Barbarosa, the great German emperor, in his war against the Turks.[3] Günther stopped at Lorelei's father's manor to beg a bite to eat. When he saw Lorelei, he was struck by her beauty, but he was too shy to speak to her, because he was nothing but a poor mercenary and she was the daughter of the manor lord. Instead, he sat quietly while she brought him food. Her kindness and gentleness impressed him even more than her beauty, and when he shyly complimented her on the meal, she paused and looked at him. Günther lingered a few days, and by the time he left for the Crusades, he carried Lorelei's love with him, symbolized by the ribbon she took from her hair and tied around his arm.[4]

Time passed slowly for Lorelei as she waited for Günther to return. A year passed, then two. Every day she prayed for his safety. Her heart and mind were full of nothing but longing for Günther's reappearance. But even as she waited, suitors kept coming. They cared little for Lorelei's pledge to the itinerant knight. In vain she begged them to stop; however, the stream of men hoping to win the beautiful Lorelei

continued. When she continued to turn them away, one young baron despaired and threw himself into the Rhine. A few months later, another followed suit, then another. The envious people in the town murmured that Lorelei was a witch, that her dazzling beauty had cast a spell that caused the young men's deaths. Others dismissed this accusation as nonsense, but they could not stop the venomous tongues. Soon charges were brought against the girl, and she was taken before the Archbishop of Köln.[5]

A tall imposing man with white hair, the Archbishop heard the charges, then glared at her from beneath bushy eyebrows. "Well, answer, girl! Have you caused these deaths by some witchery?"

"Never, Your Grace," she replied. "It is only that my heart is waiting for one who is fighting for the Holy Land. I feel for these others; I wish my face were so hideous it would never cause such harm, but my heart is given." And she told him about Günther.

"Hmmph. It seems clear to me you are waiting for a dead man. It has been more than two years, and no word? Find another love and settle down before all the young men of the land die because of you."

"Please don't force me to marry! I must wait for Günther."

"You shall wait no longer, I say. Choose, or I shall summon them here and choose for you!"

Lorelei bowed her head and sobbed, then raised her tear-filled eyes to look into the Archbishop's face.

"Will you then permit me to join the convent instead of marrying?[6] I would rather die alone, faithful to Günther, than married to a man I could never love. And in a convent, my accursed beauty would be hidden from the world of men."

Stern as he was, the Archbishop could not be unmoved by Lorelei's beautiful, tear-streaked face.

"Very well, you may join the convent."

Lorelei sadly returned home guarded by the Archbishop's men, bid her family good-bye, and set sail down the Rhine toward the convent. They passed the town of St. Goar, carefully maneuvering their skiff through the treacherous currents as the Rhine tortuously bent sharply and narrowed. Below St. Goar, a huge rock jutted out over the river. Lorelei was suddenly struck by a wish to see her father's house once more. She begged her guards to allow her to climb the cliff for one last glimpse of her childhood home.

They consented but did not climb with her, choosing to watch from the bottom as the slim figure moved slowly to the top of the boulder. As she climbed, the men observed another boat poling up the Rhine toward Köln. They watched the boat pass out of sight beyond the rock, and discussed the unenviable task of negotiating the turn going upstream. Suddenly, they heard a faint cry and looked up to see Lorelei atop the rock, jumping and waving her arms. The cliff blocked their view of the moving vessel, so they could not see what Lorelei saw at its prow: a mail-clad figure with a tattered ribbon tied around his forearm.

On his ship, Günther and his men heard her cries and looked up. Günther and Lorelei locked eyes. As his men gaped in awe at the beautiful girl, standing like an angel on the cliff above the Rhine, they forgot to steer, and in a split second the current rammed the boat against the rocky shoreline of the sharp curve. In less time than it takes to tell, the ship broke apart, and the fierce currents pulled the men under.

In horror, Lorelei realized Günther was dead, and that her beauty had been the cause. With a wild shriek, she leapt from the rock and plummeted into the Rhine.

". . . and from that day to this," Dieter's father concluded, "people have reported seeing her now and again waving from Loreleiberg. Some say she's trying to warn vessels from the rocks. Others say she's luring men to their deaths with a glimpse of her glorious face, bedazzling them and making them forget to steer until they crash against the rocky shore." Dieter's father wiped his brow as he looked back toward Loreleiberg.

"What do you say, Vati ("daddy"; FAH-tea)? Is she helping or trying to hurt us?" Dieter asked.

His father smiled. "That depends on how you look at it, Dieter. Some people see good things in the world, and others see bad. It all depends on how you look at it."

Safe in the calm waters below the curve, Dieter looked back at Loreleiberg. The sun glinted on the rock, and he wondered, as he stared at the brightness of the cliff, if he would ever see Lorelei. He couldn't decide if he hoped he would. But he knew someday, when he taught his son to steer a barge, he would tell him The Lorelei.

The Lorelei (Germany)—
Follow-Up Information and Activities

SPECIFIC CULTURAL NOTES

The following information refers to the corresponding numbers on the previous pages of the folktale. This is provided for additional insight and cultural information. Use as needed or desired.

Notes

1. The Rhine River begins at Switzerland's Lake Constance (or Bodensee, in German) and runs northward 820 miles into the North Sea in the Netherlands.

2. Tournaments were a favorite entertainment in Europe in the Age of Chivalry, as the period from 800–1400 was known. Knights hoping to win the notice of powerful nobles would compete in jousting, sword fights, and other tests of their combat skills. Often knights were killed in these fights. The knight who outlasted all challengers would be allowed to crown a queen of the tournament, an honor usually conferred on a pretty girl of noble birth, or the knight's sweetheart. Those who have read *Robin Hood* will remember that Robin crowned Maid Marion queen of the tournament.

3. A Crusade is defined as a Holy War. The Crusades (seven wars in all) began in 1096. A throng of peasants, vagabonds, and poor knights (such as Günther) led by Peter the Hermit, a French preacher with no military training, marched from Europe into Asia Minor, the area now known as Turkey. They were quickly destroyed by the Turks. Günther was on his way to join the Third Crusade, begun in 1187. Frederick I (called Frederick Barbarosa, or "red beard"), emperor of Germany from 1152 to 1190, agreed to join forces with the French King Philip II and the English King Richard the Lionhearted. The forces of the three most powerful rulers in Europe never met in the East, and Frederick drowned while swimming in a river, without ever fighting in the Crusade. The last Crusade was in 1270. More on the Crusades is provided in the background information for this story.
    Many knights like Günther (who were without a nobleman to work for or who were without land or money) tried to distinguish themselves by fighting in the Crusades. Also, there was much looting done in Asia Minor.

4. A token of love was often given between sweethearts during the Age of Chivalry. Young women would give their men a lock of hair, a hair ribbon, or some other token such as a flower to demonstrate their love and willingness to wait for the young man's return. The locket was developed from this custom.

5. The cathedral in Köln (the English name is Cologne) is one of the most impressive in Europe, and many legends exist about its origins. The archbishop at this cathedral would have been an incredibly powerful man, about as powerful as a governor in American cultures.

6. Women in twelfth-century Europe had little choice regarding what they did with their lives. They were considered the property of their fathers and husbands. Lorelei is asking for the only alternative that would be acceptable to marriage. Girls who could not attract husbands were sometimes sent to convents.

The Lorelei (Germany)—
Follow-Up Information and Activities

THE RHINE AND OTHER RIVERS

The Rhine has been described as a dangerous river, despite its gentle currents. Do you think that Lorelei's character could have been invented as a reason why so many boatmen crashed at the sharp curve in the Rhine at Loreleiberg? Do you think Lorelei really existed? Do you think the story *The Lorelei* could be a combination of a real person's existence and a need to explain why that part of the Rhine was so dangerous?

Think about famous rivers in your country. The Mississippi is a famous river in the United States, and the St. Lawrence is a famous river in Canada. How was each of these rivers important to the development of its region? How did either river affect the culture of the surrounding area? Do you live near a river that was important to the development of your region or country? Has this river influenced your cultural habits, behaviors, or beliefs in any way?

In Germany, barons and other noblemen built their castles along the Rhine for a reason: protection from attack. What strategic value can you see in building a fortress along a river? Can you find any historic examples of this in the cultural background of your region or country?

Many stories from Germany center around the Rhine. What stories do you know about a river in your area? Have there ever been any ghosts reported along its banks? Did pirates lurk in the area? Were there any massacres near the river in the early years of your country? Who sailed on the river? When?

In investigating the answers to these questions, list the most interesting facts you uncovered.

_____

_____

_____

_____

_____

_____

_____

_____

_____

_____

_____

_____

The Lorelei (Germany)—
Follow-Up Information and Activities

LORELEI AND BEAUTY

The Lorelei offers much food for thought regarding physical appearances. Cultures place different emphases on personal attractiveness. Some individuals who view themselves as unattractive often think about how great it would be if they could only be "beautiful." Some people who are considered attractive by others often see themselves as "ugly" because they can find physical flaws with their appearance. In some cultures, the development of inner character qualities is sometimes given lower priority than the improvement of one's physical appearance. How does an individual's physical appearance influence others in your culture? Have you ever made a snap judgment based on someone's looks, only to discover later that you were wrong? How does the proverb "You can't judge a book by its cover" relate to this story? How does your culture reward outer beauty in contrast to inner character?

Cultures were very different during the time of the Crusades. People now have many choices regarding the personal details of their lives, such as the kinds of relationships they will have with others and the value they place on physical and personal characteristics. Lorelei wanted to be valued for her character qualities instead of her looks. Many in her culture, however, thought that beauty was more important than any other factor. Lorelei, on the other hand, wanted "to marry someone whose affection for her would not fade with her beauty as she grew older." Think about these factors as you answer the following questions.

What qualities do you possess that might be desirable to others?

_____

_____

_____

What qualities would you seek in a future friend or partner?

_____

_____

_____

Make a list of several people you know. Beside their name, identify their best quality.

_____

_____

_____

_____

_____

_____

The Lorelei (Germany)— Follow-Up Information and Activities

CULTURAL CHOICES

Lorelei's Choices: The culture in which Lorelei lived gave her little control over many of her choices in life. She could choose to marry, or she could join a convent—but that was the extent of her options. Contrast the differences in the choices Lorelei had regarding partner selection with the choices that exist in your own culture:

_____

_____

_____

_____

_____

_____

Dieter's Choices: Dieter became a ferryman like his father. At the end of the story, he indicated that he would also teach his son to steer a barge and would tell him the story *The Lorelei*. In Dieter's culture, he had little choice about whether to follow in his father's footsteps. Contrast this with the career choices you have in your culture. Explain what choice you will have in selecting your future career. How much will your family members influence your decision? If you want a career your parents do not value, will you still be able to pursue that career? How happy are you with the career choices you have in your culture?

_____

_____

_____

_____

_____

Beyond the Story—Cultural Differences: Investigate the career and marriage choices of cultures other than the one in *The Lorelei*. How do they differ from your own? Are there choices in other cultures you wish you had in your own culture? What cultural practices did you discover that you do not wish to acquire?

_____

_____

_____

_____

_____

The Lorelei (Germany)—
Follow-Up Information and Activities

THE CRUSADES

The Crusades greatly influenced the development of European countries. What wars have been important to the development of your country? Explain.

_____

_____

_____

_____

If you had lived in the time of the Crusades, would you have wanted to fight in them? Explain why or why not.

_____

_____

_____

_____

_____

_____

_____

The Ultimate Challenge:
An Information Scavenger Hunt

The following terms represent some of the more bizarre and interesting stories from the Crusades. Look them up on a CD-ROM, in standard encyclopedias, in textbooks, or in other resources. What can you learn about these names? Write your findings on separate paper.

Knights Templar, Knights Hospitaler, Seljuks, Saracens, Byzantium, Constantinople, The Second Crusade Disaster, Philip II, Richard the Lionhearted, Prince John, The Children's Crusade

Answer Guide for
"An Information Scavenger Hunt"

THE KNIGHTS TEMPLAR

- This order was organized in 1128 to protect Christians traveling to Jerusalem. Pilgrims, as these travelers were called, often carried large amounts of money or jewels, and bandits lined the roads to Jerusalem waiting to prey on them.

- A Knight Templar was also a monk. Templars were heavily recruited during the Crusades because they were skilled warriors and pious men.

THE KNIGHTS HOSPITALER

- The Knights Hospitaler were a nursing order, organized to create a hospital in Jerusalem for crusaders and pilgrims. Although knights and warriors, these men cared for the sick and dying of the Crusades.

- Read a modern-language version of Chaucer's **The Canterbury Tales** to learn more about pilgrims and knights in the age of the Crusades.

THE SELJUKS

- The Seljuks were Turks who united several small Arab countries into one kingdom during the eleventh century. The resulting Arab nation had a powerful army and bordered the Byzantine Empire.

- This united Arab nation frightened the Byzantine emperor, Alexius I. He assumed that it would be simply a matter of time before the Seljuks attacked him, so he appealed for help to Western Europe, comprising mostly France, England, Germany, and Austria.

- Alexius knew that the kings of Western Europe might not care if his country were attacked, but they did care about Jerusalem. He sent word that the Arabs had occupied Jerusalem and would probably not allow pilgrims to visit there. This got the results he wanted, and a band of crusaders set out to free the Holy City.

- The Seljuks were Muslim. They considered Jerusalem a Holy City and were determined to hold out as the first wave of crusaders reached it. But in June 1099, the crusaders captured the city. The slaughter of the defeated Seljuks was so great that one crusader wrote in his diary, "the knights rode in blood up to their horses' knees." The Seljuks never forgot the massacre of 1099.

THE SARACENS

- The Saracens were also Arabs, with reputations as fierce raiders. They were subjugated by the Seljuks before the Crusades. Christian Europeans made little distinction between a Seljuk Arab and a Saracen Arab.

- Read about Arab history and culture in your local library. Look up Saracens, Seljuks, Crusades, or Arab History.

BYZANTIUM (THE BYZANTINE EMPIRE)

- The Byzantine Empire covered the area we now know as Turkey.

- It was ruled by an emperor.

- Although it was Christian, there were philosophical differences between Christianity as practiced in the Byzantine Empire and in Western Europe. This contributed to what happened to Constantinople during the Fourth Crusade.

CONSTANTINOPLE

- Constantinople was the capital of the Byzantine Empire.

- In the Fourth Crusade, the crusaders, not the Seljuks, attacked Constantinople.

- Constantinople was renamed Istanbul in 1930.

- There are many interesting books about the Crusades in your library. Look up Byzantine Empire, Crusades, Pope Innocent III, or Constantinople.

THE SECOND CRUSADE DISASTER

- The Turkish Prince Nureddin led an attack in 1146 to regain the land the Arabs lost in the First Crusade and to get revenge for the bloody massacre.

- The Second Crusade began in 1147 when crusaders arrived to take Jerusalem back from Nureddin's forces. The crusaders were overconfident, remembering the First Crusade.

- The Second Crusade hurt the Byzantine Empire more than the Arabs ever did. German and French troops began to plunder Byzantine towns along the way to Jerusalem.

- Conrad III of Germany and Louis VII of France, the two kings leading the Second Crusade, hated each other and refused to cooperate. Instead of joining forces to fight the Arabs, the French and Germans operated separately and were destroyed by Arab forces.

PHILIP II (PHILIP AUGUSTUS)

- Philip, the King of the French, had only one eye.

- He pretended to be an ally of King Richard the Lionhearted (the king of England) in the Third Crusade. Secretly he plotted with Richard's younger brother, Prince John, who ruled England while Richard was away fighting.

- When Richard was captured and held for ransom on his way home from the Crusades, Philip and John worked together to try to keep the ransom from being paid.

- Prince John is a prominent character in the story of Robin Hood. Read it to learn more about life in England during the Crusades.

RICHARD THE LIONHEARTED (RICHARD COEUR DE LION)

- Richard was king of England for ten years, yet he lived in England for only six months of that time.

- He spoke French as his first language.

- Richard was captured on his way home from the Third Crusade by an Austrian king and held for ransom. English noblemen, disgusted with the weak rule of Prince John, paid for Richard's release.

- As revenge on Philip II, Richard launched a war against France. His troops captured a significant amount of French land.

- King Richard was wounded during a battle and died soon afterward. Prince John became king of England.

PRINCE JOHN

- John was a poor military leader, and Philip of France recaptured all the lands he had lost to King Richard. (One of these regions was called Normandy, which later became the site of a famous World War II battle.)

- John spent so much money trying to fight Philip that he had to impose increasingly heavy taxes on his people to keep his armies going. The nobles grumbled and finally refused to pay after a devastating loss in 1214.

- John was in a weak position when the nobility revolted. If his noblemen did not pay their taxes, he could not pay the bills for the army's food and other needs. He tried to put down the rebellion, but the nobles were stronger and richer. John had to agree to their demands.

- John met with the noblemen in 1215 and signed a document known as the Magna Carta (Great Charter). It listed several rights guaranteed to all English nobility, such as the right to a trial by a jury of their peers. The Magna Carta was a list of what the king was and was not allowed to do at that time. It would become an inspiration for the U.S. Declaration of Independence. King John had no idea, when he signed the Magna Carta in 1215, that he would be aiding a revolt against English power 561 years later, when the North American colonies rebelled and formed the United States of America in 1776.

THE CHILDREN'S CRUSADE

- The Children's Crusade began in 1212 when two teenage boys began to preach the same message, each unaware of the other's existence. One boy preached in France, the other in Germany.

- Each said that the first three Crusades failed because the crusaders did not lead holy, innocent lives. A holy war could be won only by holy, innocent warriors. Who, the boys asked, could be more innocent than children?

- Two groups of children followed these boy preachers and, each group unaware of the other, set off for the Holy Land.

- The German band reached the coast of Italy but could not find any ships willing to take them across the Mediterranean Sea. Some children remained in Italy, but most walked back to Germany.

- The French group marched to Marseilles, a city on the coast of France. They arranged for passage to the Holy Land with a group of merchants, but as soon as they had the children on board, the merchants sailed to Egypt and sold every child into slavery.

- The Children's Crusade is considered one of history's most bizarre events.

The Lorelei (Germany)—
Wrap-Up Activity

GAME SHOW FUN

To leaders of the game show activities: Use the following questions in your favorite game show format. (See page xv for activity suggestions.) These questions may be shown on an overhead projector or prepared as separate cards. For an easier round of questions, include the four choices of answers. For a more challenging experience, use only the question stem (without the choices of answers). The questions relate to the story content only. (Answers appear on page xvi.) Additional questions may be prepared from the specific cultural information provided in this section or discovered by the involved learners.

Questions

1. *The Lorelei* was first told to eleven-year-old Dieter by his father as they approached a huge rock. What was this rock called?

   A. Rhine

   B. Rhineberg

   C. Lorelei

   D. Loreleiberg

2. As they floated down the Rhine in their barge, Dieter's father suddenly shouted "Achtung!" What does *Achtung* mean?

   A. Someone sneezed

   B. Pay attention

   C. Pirates are about to attack the ship

   D. A dangerous bird is flying near

3. Many suitors wanted to marry Lorelei. What is a suitor?

   A. A person who sews for others

   B. Someone who dresses very formally

   C. Someone who courts a woman

   D. A person who tries to please others

4. What did Lorelei think about her own beauty?

   A. She was happy that it caused so many men to fall in love with her.

   B. Despite her looks, she didn't think she was pretty enough.

   C. It caused her to treat the less attractive girls disrespectfully.

   D. She viewed her beauty as a disadvantage.

5. How did Lorelei feel about the many men she refused to marry?

   A. She felt pity for them.

   B. She laughed in their face.

   C. She ordered them to be executed.

   D. She hoped even more suitors would pursue her.

6. Why did Lorelei reject so many men who wanted to marry her?

   A. Her religious beliefs prevented her from marrying.

   B. She wanted to wait until a wealthier man proposed.

   C. She wanted someone who would still love her after her beauty faded.

   D. She wanted to marry someone who met the approval of both her mother and father.

7. Why wasn't Lorelei free to choose her own husband?

   A. She was too young to make such a decision.

   B. The customs at that time didn't allow women to choose a mate.

   C. Her father was afraid she would select the wrong man.

   D. Mates were chosen only according to the amount of money they offered the family.

8. When they first met, why didn't Günther openly express his love for Lorelei and ask her to marry him?

   A. He was going to battle soon and didn't want to pursue her until after he returned.

   B. He had already proposed marriage to another girl before he met Lorelei.

   C. He was too shy, and he felt that he was too poor to ask for her hand in marriage.

   D. He was afraid that the other knights would be jealous enough to kill him.

9. What physical symbol did Günther wear as his reminder of Lorelei's love?

   A. One of her hair ribbons

   B. A friendship ring

   C. A red carnation

   D. A tattoo with the words "Lovely Lorelei"

10. After Lorelei had rejected so many suitors, what accusation did some of the envious townspeople make that forced her to endure a trial?

   A. They said she was murdering the town's bachelors by pushing them off a cliff.

   B. They accused her of being a witch.

   C. They said her beauty caused all of the other available young maidens to give up their hopes of finding a husband.

   D. They accused her of causing ships to sink.

11. What did Lorelei ask the Archbishop to let her do instead of marrying someone she didn't love?

   A. Go to jail

   B. Jump off a cliff

   C. Join a group that was fighting in the Crusades

   D. Join the convent

12. Why did Lorelei ask the guards to stop as they were sailing down the Rhine toward the convent?

    A. She planned to jump to her death.

    B. She wanted to run away from the guards.

    C. She wanted to walk to the top of the cliff to see if Günther was sailing toward her town.

    D. She wanted one last glimpse of her childhood home.

13. Why did Lorelei jump to her death?

    A. She didn't want to join the convent.

    B. She didn't want to marry someone she didn't love.

    C. She was trying to rescue Günther.

    D. She realized she had caused Günther's death.

14. Why did skilled ferrymen have such difficulty when they approached Loreleiberg?

    A. The ghost of Lorelei frightened them.

    B. The required upstream turn demanded extreme skill.

    C. Turbulent weather often made the passage treacherous.

    D. Water fairies temporarily hypnotized the ferrymen.

15. According to the legend, why does Lorelei "reappear" occasionally?

    A. To warn approaching vessels of the dangerous sharp rocks

    B. To look for her lost Günther

    C. To lure men to their death

    D. Both A and C

Chapter 4

Clever Peter and the *Sultan*

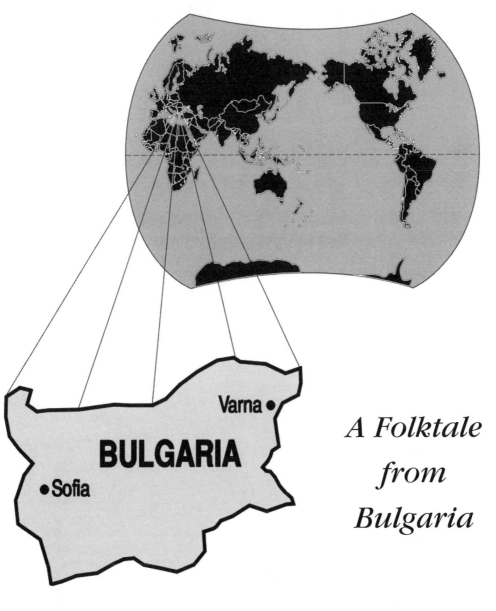

A Folktale from Bulgaria

About the Contributor

This section was prepared primarily by

Priscilla Howe

In 1988 Priscilla Howe left her job as a Slavic librarian at the University of Kansas, thinking that she'd never use her fluency in the Bulgarian language again. Not so! Priscilla looks for and tells stories from all over the world, sometimes in other languages, including Bulgarian. Some of her stories for adults draw on her experiences living in Bulgaria in 1983–1984.

Priscilla has been telling stories since 1988 (full-time since 1993). She tells folktales, original stories, and stories from books to listeners of all ages around the United States and in Europe, as well as to her cat, Joe Fish, at home in Lawrence, Kansas.

Priscilla is also searching for the best pie on earth.

Clever Peter and the Sultan (Bulgaria)— Cultural Background

GLOSSARY AND PRONUNCIATION GUIDE

The words that follow are used in the story *Clever Peter and the Sultan*. Refer to this list as needed for the correct pronunciations and meanings.

Bulgarian Word	Pronunciation Suggestions	Meaning of the Word in Bulgarian
boza	bo-ZAH	fermented millet drink
dzhezveh	JEZ-veh	Turkish coffee pot
kalpak	coll-POCK	cylindrical hat
kisselo mlyako	KEY-sell-o MLYACK-oh	yogurt
lukanka	loo-CONK-ah	salami
lyutenitsa	LYOO-ten-eat-sah	spicy tomato spread
Martenitsi	MAR-tin-eat-see	tassel worn on March 1st
pitka	PEAT-kah	flat round bread
sireneh	SEAR-en-eh	feta cheese
sultan	sool-TAN	king
survachki	suhr-VOTCH-key	decorated sticks for New Year's Day
tsurvuli	sir-VOO-lee	pointy-toed leather shoes

EXPLORING BULGARIAN CULTURE

Before experiencing the story *Clever Peter and the Sultan*, have fun with the following activity. In the left portion of the boxes that follow are questions about your culture. Write your answers in the provided spaces. Then contrast your answers with those at the right describing the same experiences in the Bulgarian culture.

If you were writing a story that needed a powerful leader as a major character, what position would you choose for that leader? Tell why.

Answer: _____

_____

_____

_____

_____

_____

_____

The Sultan was the position chosen as the leader in this story about Clever Peter. (The position of a sultan is similar to that of a king in some cultures.) Bulgaria is a small country in Eastern Europe, first founded as a country in the year 681. For almost five hundred years (from the 1300s until the 1800s), Bulgaria was under the rule of the Turks of the Ottoman Empire. Because of this, there is considerable Turkish influence in the culture and language. In this story the Sultan is Turkish; the Bulgarians had a czar (king) before and after the Turkish rule until the middle of the twentieth century. A different version of this story has a czar instead of a sultan. (There is still a Turkish minority in Bulgaria today, as well as a small Gypsy population.)

Note: The Slavic term *czar* is a corrupted form of the Roman *Caesar*.

Do you celebrate New Year's Day, Valentine's Day, or Halloween in your culture? If so, tell how you celebrate each one. If not, describe how you celebrate your favorite holiday.

Answer: _____

_____

_____

_____

_____

_____

On New Year's Day, Bulgarians decorate with *survachki*—sticks about a yard long from the cornel cherry tree that are decorated with colored paper, popcorn, and berries. They hit adults (gently) with these sticks, and the adults are given a coin in exchange, as a kind of reverse "trick or treat." (Bulgarians don't celebrate Halloween.) In the beginning of March, Bulgarians give each other *Martenitsi* (little red and white tassels to pin to their clothes for good fortune and friendship). Children and adults give *Martenitsi* to their friends in a manner similar to the giving of valentines by those who celebrate Valentine's Day.

If you were packing a supply of food for yourself for a full day of travel, describe what you would prepare.

Answer: _____

_____

_____

In this story, Clever Peter packed a *pitka, sireneh,* and a bottle of *boza*. A *pitka* is a round flat loaf of bread, *sireneh* is feta cheese, and *boza* is a fermented millet drink. (Millet is a type of grass cultivated for its grain.) In Bulgaria today, mostly children and nursing mothers drink *boza,* which is rich in the B vitamins. Bulgarian food is similar in many respects to Greek food.

If you were dressing up to look old-fashioned, what might you choose to wear on your head and on your feet?

Answer: _____

_____

_____

_____

_____

_____

_____

Clever Peter is a character who looked old-fashioned. He wore a *kalpak* on his head and *tsurvuli* on his feet. *Tsurvuli* are thick leather shoes with toes that curl up. They lace up around thick leggings. Before shoes were made in factories in Bulgaria, practically all men wore *tsurvuli*. A *kalpak* is a black cylindrical hat that looks much like a fez. Today only a few older men in the villages of Bulgaria wear *kalpaks*.

Assume that you are taking a ride through the countryside nearest you. Would you see any produce growing? Describe any workers you might see in action.

Answer: _____

_____

_____

_____

_____

Bulgaria produces many agricultural products, including grapes for wine and attar of roses for some of the finest perfume houses in Paris. A festival held in the Valley of the Roses, when the rose petals are gathered, is famous throughout Bulgaria.

Describe the beverage that the adults you know drink most frequently.

Answer: _____

_____

_____

_____

_____

Bulgarians (as well as Turks and Greeks) drink Turkish coffee, a very strong, hot beverage made in a copper pot called a *dzhezveh*. It is served in little cups, and the dregs are left in the cup. Some Bulgarians read fortunes in these coffee grounds.

If you could not utter a sound, how could you communicate the word *no* just by moving your head? What about the word *yes*?

Answer: _____

_____

_____

_____

Body language can be quite different among cultures. Sometimes a gesture in one culture can have an opposite meaning in another culture. When Bulgarians say *yes*, they move their heads from side to side, and when they say *no*, they nod their heads up and down. An especially strong *no* is a quick nod upward, accompanied by a tongue click. This can be confusing at first to visitors from other cultures.

Clever Peter and the Sultan

A Folktale from Bulgaria

Retold by Priscilla Howe

Bulgaria was under the rule of the Ottoman Empire for five hundred years, resulting in many of their stories having a distinctly Eastern flavor. Clever Peter (Khitur Petur) is, however, truly Bulgarian. Bulgarians are proud of this trickster. In the city of Gabrovo, near the Museum of Humor, is a statue of Clever Peter.

Long ago, a Sultan in the Ottoman Empire was bored. Day after boring day passed with nothing more interesting happening than flies buzzing in the hot sun. Finally the Sultan sent out a messenger to all of Eastern Europe, saying that if any man could tell a lie that the Sultan could not believe, he would give that liar two sacks of gold.

All the best fibbers in the land traveled to Constantinople to try their luck. They all told their biggest "windies" to the Sultan, but they all left in disgrace. The Sultan remained bored.

Clever Peter, too, was bored. By the time word of the challenge arrived at his village in Bulgaria, the children were no longer decorating *survachki,* and the time for *Martenitsi* had passed. Clever Peter dressed, tied his *tsurvuli,* and put his best kalpak on his head. He packed a meal of *pitka* and *sireneh* with a little bottle of *boza,* kissed his wife good-bye, and rode off on his old donkey. He passed fields of lavender, fields of roses, orchards, and vineyards. Both men and women worked in these fields, and they waved to Clever Peter as he rode by.

"Ey, Peter, where are you going?"

"I'm off to see the Sultan."

"Why don't you have big sacks to collect the gold, Peter?"

"If the Sultan wants to give me gold, he can give me the sacks as well!"

When Clever Peter arrived at the Sultan's palace, he was ushered directly in to see the Sultan, who was sitting on many cushions drinking Turkish coffee.

"I suppose you are going to tell me a lie," sneered the Sultan.

"In truth, I've come to collect the money your father owed my father. Years ago, your father borrowed two bushels of gold from my father and never paid it back."

"No!" screamed the Sultan, with a quick upward nod of his head and a click of his tongue. "My father was the Sultan! He would never borrow money from a peasant like *your* father!"

"You don't believe me? Are you saying I'm a liar?"

The Sultan's face turned pink, then red. He puffed his cheeks out and clenched his fists, but Peter had him. If he agreed that Peter was telling the truth, then the Sultan owed him two bushels of gold. But if he knew it was a lie and accepted it, then the Sultan owed Peter only two sacks full for the lie.

Clever Peter rode his donkey home with two sacks of gold, telling everyone he met how he had tricked the Sultan. And the Sultan? He had stopped being bored, at least for a while.

64

Clever Peter and the Sultan (Bulgaria)— Follow-Up Information and Activities

FUN WITH CLEVER PETER

After experiencing the story *Clever Peter and the Sultan,* review the background concepts (provided earlier) for a discussion of how these ideas related to the story. Several additional Bulgarian customs may be of interest to you. Consider the thoughts in the following boxes.

Think about some gestures you use in your daily life, such as the "thumbs up" signal or the "high five" sign as a greeting. Identify and describe three other gestures you use to communicate a feeling, thought, or emotion. Would foreigners understand each of these three gestures? Why or why not?

Answer: (Use extra paper, if needed.)

_____

_____

The gestures for *no* and *yes* are different for Bulgarians, as are several other gestures in their culture. For example, they don't cross their fingers to wish someone luck; instead, they press a thumb against the outside of an index finger. To call someone to them, they'll point the whole hand at them (flat) and wave up and down.

Do you eat peanut butter (and jelly), yogurt, or black olives? If so, tell how often you eat them and how they might be prepared.

Answer: _____

_____

_____

_____

_____

_____

_____

_____

_____

_____

Most Bulgarians love to eat and drink. They don't eat peanut butter and jelly, however. Instead, the children eat a slightly spicy tomato spread called *lyutenitsa.* Even though peanuts are sold on the street (both salted and roasted), peanut butter is unknown in Bulgaria. Bulgarian children don't drink milk, but they do eat yogurt (called *kisselo mlyako* or sour milk). The yogurt is not flavored, but sometimes sugar is added. Not only do Bulgarians eat yogurt made from cow's milk, but sheep yogurt is also available in the spring. Bulgarians eat spicy food with a dollop of yogurt on the side to cool the heat. Feta cheese (a white cheese made from cow's or sheep's milk) is common in both Bulgaria and Greece. Sometimes it is eaten with black olives and a special salami called *lukanka.* Their meals almost always are served with some type of bread.

Where would you choose to travel for a vacation in your own country? Tell why.

Answer: (Use extra paper, if needed.)

_____

_____

_____

_____

There are two main vacation spots in Bulgaria: the Black Sea coast and the mountains. Bulgaria is a popular tourist spot today in Eastern Europe because of the beaches, ski resorts, and hiking trails. On sunny days in the spring and summer, city dwellers in Sofia ride the ski lift or take the bus to the top of Mount Vitosha for picnics and hiking.

Clever Peter and the Sultan (Bulgaria)— Wrap-Up Activity

GAME SHOW FUN

To leaders of the game show activities: Use the following questions in your favorite game show format. (See page xv for activity suggestions.) These questions may be shown on an overhead projector or prepared as separate cards. For an easier round of questions, include the four choices of answers. For a more challenging experience, use only the question stem (without the choices of answers). The questions relate to the story content only. (Answers appear on page xvi.) Additional questions may be prepared from the specific cultural information provided in this section or discovered by the involved learners.

Questions from the Story Content

1. What was the reward for telling the Sultan a lie that he would have to believe?

    A. The hand of his daughter in marriage

    B. Two sacks of gold

    C. Two loaves of *pitka*

    D. Two bushels of *Martenitsi*

2. Why did the Sultan issue the challenge about the lie?

    A. He thought that hearing a good lie might temporarily relieve his boredom.

    B. He imagined that giving away some of his gold would make him feel better.

    C. He thought it would help him find the man from whom he had borrowed money many years earlier.

    D. He wanted to ridicule and laugh at the poor men who responded to his challenge.

3. Why didn't the Sultan believe that his own father could have borrowed money from Peter's father?

    A. The age difference in the two men was too great for this to have happened.

    B. The Sultan only borrowed money from neighboring rulers.

    C. The Sultan's father had always been too wealthy to need anyone else's money.

    D. Sultans didn't generally borrow money from those of a much lower class.

4. Why was Clever Peter able to trick the Sultan?

    A. The Sultan had been so bored for so long that he was ready to believe Peter's story.

    B. The Sultan had been drinking some *boza* and was unable to fully comprehend what Peter was telling him.

    C. The Sultan could not say Peter's story was true, or he would owe Peter two *bushels* of gold instead of the smaller amount of two *sacks* of gold he had offered to a successful liar.

    D. The Sultan had been told so many lies by the great numbers of men who had responded to his challenge that he was becoming too befuddled to outwit Peter.

5. What did the Sultan do when he realized he had been tricked by a clever man?

    A. He laughed so hard that he decided to double the reward.

    B. He kept his word and gave the reward.

    C. He was so angry about being tricked that he had his guards remove Peter from his kingdom.

    D. He offered Peter a job in his palace.

Questions About Vocabulary Terms from the Story

6. The Sultan in the story issued a challenge to the townspeople. What is a Sultan?

    A. A major ruler (such as a king)

    B. A liar

    C. A storyteller

    D. A person who broadcasts the news to all of the villagers

7. When Peter began his journey, he put on his best *kalpak*. What would most Americans likely wear instead of a *kalpak*?

   A. A book bag

   B. A wind-resistant overcoat

   C. Sunglasses

   D. A hat or a cap

8. The travelers to Constantinople told their best "windies" to the Sultan. What is a "windie"?

   A. A story accompanied by a wind instrument

   B. An untruth

   C. A factual lecture about the weather

   D. A top secret that can be shared only with someone of a high rank

9. Peter's father was referred to as a peasant. What is a peasant?

   A. A large, long-tailed, and brightly colored bird

   B. An uneducated person of low social status

   C. A happy, cheery person who is almost always in a good mood

   D. A member of an opposing political party

10. Children in Bulgaria decorate *survachki*. During which holiday do they use them?

    A. Halloween

    B. Valentine's Day

    C. New Year's Day

    D. April Fool's Day

Questions About Bulgaria and Its Culture

11. American children frequently eat peanut butter and jelly sandwiches at snack time. What would many Bulgarian children likely eat instead?

    A. A slightly spicy tomato spread called *lyutenitsa*

    B. Either french fries or onion rings

    C. Bulgarian meat called lukana

    D. Sliced fruit prepared in a *dzhezveh*

12. Each culture has its own unique body language. In this story the sultan gave a quick upward nod of his head and a click of his tongue. In the Bulgarian culture, what does this communicate?

    A. Hello

    B. Good-bye

    C. Yes

    D. No

13. When Bulgarian children hit the adults with their *survachki* sticks, what do they get in return?

    A. Candy

    B. A coin

    C. A rose

    D. Bread

14. Why is Bulgaria a popular tourist spot in Eastern Europe?

    A. There are numerous shopping malls with very low prices on most products.

    B. Most of the restaurants specialize in outstanding, mouth-watering cuisine.

    C. The beaches, ski resorts, and hiking trails are attractive to visitors.

    D. The area hosts several major festivals and conventions.

15. What is one main difference in how coffee is served in Bulgaria from how it is typically served in most American cultures?

    A. Coffee is served only in the late evenings.

    B. The only acceptable time to enjoy coffee is after a meal has completely ended.

    C. The coffee dregs are left in the cups.

    D. Coffee is served to young students in most schools during break time.

Chapter 5

Pacala

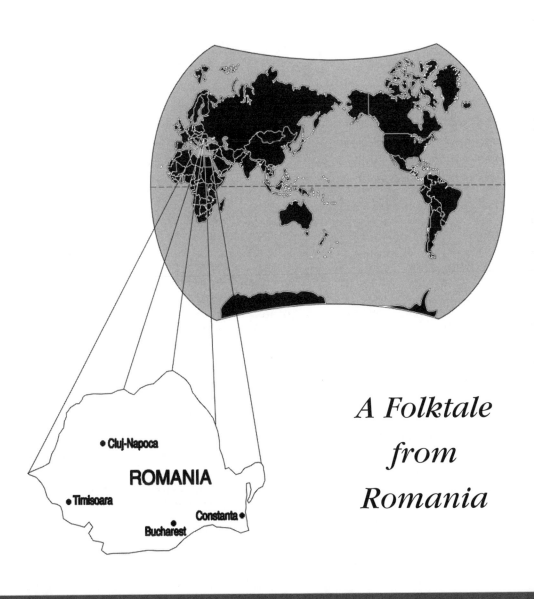

ROMANIA

● Cluj-Napoca

● Timisoara

Bucharest ● Constanta ●

A Folktale from Romania

About the Contributor

This section was prepared primarily by

Sam yada Cannarozzi

Sam yada Cannarozzi, sometimes known as the melting-pot storyteller, is of Sicilian and Yugoslavian heritage. He and Margrethe Højlund, Danish actress and storyteller, have two trilingual children, with whom they live near Lyons, France. Sam graduated cum laude with a bachelor of science degree in languages and linguistics (French and German) from Georgetown University in Washington, D.C. He spent his junior year at the University of Dijon, Burgundy, then returned to France where he has lived since 1974.

Following his performance at the 1982 International Storytelling Festival, sponsored by the Center for World Cultures in Paris, Sam began to forge his own brand of oral tradition and has been telling stories since then to all types of audiences. His storytelling creations include works centering on Native American sign language, worldwide string figures, origami, and various types of poetry. He created a program of Rainbow myths and also recounts the tales of the trickster figure Till Eulenspiegel in German and English. He is also a published poet and a sound poet. He regularly tours Africa as well as France and other parts of Europe under the auspices of the United States Cultural Services.

Pacala (Romania)—Cultural Background

ROMANIA'S STORIES AND TALES

Folktale Characters

Major characters of specific cultures generally have several common traits. The character in the story *Pacala* is one of many found in Romanian folklore. Stan Bolovan, a contrasting folktale character who also preserves the traits of the Romanian spirit, is more an epic hero. Somewhat stoic, he frequently engages in battles with dragons. Pacala is a much more popular folk hero. His stories and adventures have been told for generations, and he shares definite similarities with other folktale characters in the same area of Eastern Europe and elsewhere. He would likely feel right at home listening to the stories about Germany's Till Eulenspiegel or Scandinavia's Esben Aeskefejs. He might also enjoy the folklore hero Nasreddin Odjah, who has directly influenced Romania and the surrounding European countries since the thirteenth century. (One of  Nasreddin's stories is included in this collection.) These characters, like Pacala, were always admired by the people for their campaigns against injustice, often in the form of ridicule of authority.

As is often the case with such characters, Pacala was the youngest of three brothers. Frequently the youngest and weakest often turns out to be the cleverest and most intelligent. Pacala is not only a comic figure, but also one who shows how the disadvantaged in society can triumph by using their wits. He mocks all authoritarian figures when they deserve it—the merchants, the government, and even the church—as is the case with the story presented here.

The Pacala Cycle

The story on the following pages was taken from a series of relatively short, humorous stories still told today in modern Romania. They are referred to as the Pacala Cycle. Pacala has his own special brand of foolishness—it might even be considered philosophical foolishness at times. The butt of Pacala's jokes and of the antics in this story is a minister. Romanians are not particularly an anticlerical people; in fact, they are quite religious, especially in their Orthodox faith. But abuses of power and strength do occur, as happens in this story about a cruel and stingy minister. Pacala arrives to denounce such practices wherever he finds them. Although no saint himself, Pacala's cunning bravery makes him a much appreciated image of popular belief.

A PERSONAL NOTE FROM SAM YADA CANNAROZZI

In September 1994 I was invited to Constanta, Romania, on the shores of the Black Sea, to participate in an international poetry symposium. This symposium finished with a three-day tour of Transylvania, at which time we visited some of Romania's most beautiful and historically relevant landscape. During that three-day bus ride, as well as during the symposium proper, we were graciously assisted by friends and organizers of the event. I became quick friends with Florina Dobrescu. She is a professor who lives with her husband and daughter in Constanta. Florina taught me some traditional folk songs in Romanian. I asked her if she knew any stories. She immediately responded with Pacala stories. She told them to me simply in French, but I asked her to tell them in Romanian as well so I could experience the intonations and musicality of the language. This sharing occurred very informally during the bus ride. She agreed to send me the written stories, which I later translated both from her printed copies and from my memory of her earlier vocal deliveries. She seemed shyly hesitant to be acknowledged for her contributions to this project; however, I explained that each individual puts something personal into the retelling and adaptation of a story. She related the stories; I only translated them. (In telling them, I now leave my own mark.) Her modest reaction was in the true spirit of the oral tradition. Stories really belong to everyone, even if they come from specific cultures.

GLOSSARY AND PRONUNCIATION INFORMATION

The teller or reader of this folktale either may omit the Romanian words or may add extra cultural flavor and pronounce them as they occur in the story. The story language is crafted in a manner for easy omission or inclusion and also to indicate obvious meanings for all of the Romanian words and phrases. For those who choose to include them, the following information may be of assistance:

Pacala—The main character of the story (puh-KAH-luh)

era odatà—A Romanian story beginning similar to "Once upon a time" (AIR-ruh oh-DAH-tuh)

popa—A minister (POE-puh)

a taea varfula nasului—Means "cut off the end of his nose" (uh tah-EE-uh var-FUH-lah nah-sue-LOO-ee)

paine ši branza—Means "bread and cheese" (PAH-een she-BRAHN-zah)

mielule—Means "sheep" (mie-AY-loo-lay)

un fluier—Means "flute" (oon fluh-IE-er)

tare ši moale—Means "hard and soft" (TAH-ray she mow-A-lay)

Pacala

A Folktale from Romania

As Recounted to Sam yada Cannarozzi by Florina Dobrescu

Once upon a time—or as you would say in Romania, *era odatà* (in the time of never)—wolves smoked pipes and bears made soap so good that women rubbed their cheeks and old men rubbed their beards and chins with it.

At about that same time there lived a rather puckish sort of lad named Pacala. He enjoyed kidding around, and although he was very young, he had a keen sense of justice. He could also use cleverness to get himself out of difficult situations. That's why Pacala accepted a job one day in the house of a *popa,* a minister.

This popa, however, was unlike others of his profession. Instead of being kind and caring, he was known for his cruelty and stinginess. The work agreement required Pacala to serve the popa for one year. Pacala would be paid handsomely at the end of that year, provided he never once complained about anything. Should he complain about anything at all, he would be paid nothing and the popa would have the right to *a taea varfula nasului,* or cut off the end of his nose! Pacala agreed, but only on the condition that the popa himself would also lose the end of his own nose if he ever complained about anything. And the haughty man agreed.

On the first day the popa sent Pacala to the fields to harvest grain. But he sent him off without anything to eat, thinking that would anger him enough to complain and break the contract. Pacala harvested the grain all day—then sold it for enough money to buy himself a good meal. The master fumed!

"Are you complaining?" asked Pacala.

The popa didn't answer, but he went off in a huff.

The following morning he gave Pacala *paine ši branza,* a loaf of bread and a piece of cheese to eat, but he insisted that Pacala bring the bread and cheese back at the end of the day. By lunchtime, Pacala was very hungry. He thought and thought. Finally he had an idea about how to have a good meal and still return the food he was given. When Pacala returned home that night, the popa smirked when he saw the bread and cheese.

"Did you have a good lunch, boy?" he asked.

"Oh, yes," answered Pacala, "quite fine. And here are the bread and cheese you gave me."

75

But when the popa took them, he noticed they weighed almost nothing. Then he saw a small hole in the cheese and another one in the end of the loaf of bread. Pacala had emptied them and returned the empty shapes. The popa bit his tongue to keep from complaining.

Next the cruel man sent Pacala off to pasture his *mielule,* his sheep. Pacala found a grassy field, sat under a tree while the sheep were pasturing, and began to play his *fluier,* his flute. Was it a magical flute? No one knows, but Pacala played so beautifully that the sheep all began to dance and dance and dance. They couldn't stop. They danced the entire day. Pacala played his flute the next day, and again the sheep danced. They danced all the next day, and the next. The popa noticed that his sheep were so tired at night they could hardly enter the stable. He decided to spy on Pacala to find out why. He soon discovered the magical flute that made the sheep dance.

Suddenly the evil man jumped from his hiding place and shouted, "I've caught you now!"

But Pacala simply answered, "I think that you too would like to dance." He began playing his flute again. Against his will, the popa danced in the middle of the flock all afternoon long.

Although he was exhausted, the evil man knew a miracle when he saw one. He invited Pacala to play for his wife that night. Pacala went to the man's house and began playing. The wife, who was in the attic at the time, heard the beautiful music and began dancing. She danced and danced. When she danced too close to the attic steps, she fell all the way down them and broke several bones. The popa was so angry he almost shouted in complaint—but he didn't. And even the suffering of his wife didn't soften him.

The evil master spent the entire night trying to devise a trap that would anger Pacala enough to complain and thus lose his nose.

The following morning he ordered Pacala to build a bridge across the courtyard in front of his house. "Make this bridge," he said, "so that when I cross it I will feel something hard with my first step, but with my second step I will feel something soft. Then hard, then soft . . . *tare ši moale.*"

Pacala started to work right away. When the man was occupied with other matters, Pacala slaughtered the entire flock of sheep. He positioned one sheep with its backbone up, the next with its belly up—backbone, belly, backbone, belly—until all the sheep were lined up across the courtyard.

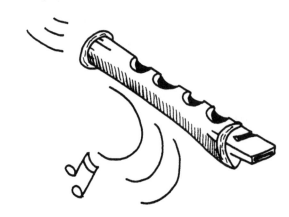

When the popa came out of his house and saw the tragedy, he clenched his hands and teeth so hard that it forced tears from his eyes. But still he didn't give in. He said nothing.

He knew he had to get away from Pacala for a while, so he decided to leave on a trip with his son. They packed several sacks for their journey. Pacala saw what was happening and hid in one of their sacks that contained religious books. As they were crossing the river, Pacala spoke in a loud and solemn voice, "Lift the sack higher. I'm getting wet."

The man and his son thought it was miraculous that the holy books could talk, so they hurried across the river to look inside the sack. When Pacala jumped out, the evil man was furious. Yet he didn't complain. He knew he would have to get rid of the troublemaker, so he decided to have his own son throw Pacala into the river that night and leave him to drown.

Pacala overheard the plan, and after the man and his son were asleep, he exchanged places with the son. Much later the popa got up in the darkness and awakened Pacala—thinking it was his own son.

"Quickly tie him up and throw him into the river!" he instructed, pointing to his sleeping son.

Following the man's orders, Pacala bound and gagged the son, put him in the sack, and carried him toward the river away from the camp. But instead of drowning him, he tied him to a distant boulder, for he had no quarrel with the son.

The man was surprised to find his son missing the next morning, but he was even more surprised to see Pacala calmly eating breakfast.

"Where is my son?" he screamed.

"Why, you yourself came to me late last night and told me to throw him in the river. Could he possibly have drowned by now?"

The popa was enraged. Pacala had ruined his house, his flock, his business, and his life. He was responsible for the suffering of his wife and son. He had ridiculed him constantly. The man could control himself no longer. He began shaking in anger!

"What's the matter," asked Pacala. "Do you have anything to complain about?"

"Yes!" he roared. "Everything you have done is horrible!"

"Well, I guess you have broken the bargain." And with that, Pacala took out his knife and cut off the tip of the man's nose.

"That will teach you," said Pacala with glee, for he knew the evil man had already cut off the noses of two other boys who had worked hard for him. The popa had cheated the boys out of their pay after tormenting them into complaining.

Who were those other boys? They were Pacala's own brothers.

Pacala, the trickster, that funny fellow, had many more adventures in his life. Perhaps I will tell you some more one day. But for now, I'll just jump into my saddle after having told you this story.

Pacala (Romania)—
Follow-Up Information and Activities

THE GEOGRAPHY AND CULTURE OF ROMANIA

Transylvania: When most people hear the word *Transylvania* (still a present-day province of Romania), they immediately think of Dracula. This historic person's real name was Vlad Dracul. He never practiced vampirism. Although at times this nobleman was a cruel warrior, he is still held in high esteem in Romania as a national hero because of his defense of the country against invaders. But that is an entirely different story....

Size and Location: Romania is a very old land of fewer than a thousand square miles (about half the size of Texas) with a population of about 22 million people. The Romanian capital is Bucaresti (Bucharest). The country's name provides a clue to its old age: Romania, from "Roman." Romania was a Roman province during pre-Christian times. There are still vestiges of an ancient Roman port in the city of Constanta on the Black Sea. The delta of the Donav (Danube) River also flows into the Black Sea, and the Danube itself serves as Romania's southern border with Bulgaria.

Language: Romania is surrounded by Russia to the east, Bulgaria to the south, and Hungary and Yugoslavia to the west, and all (with the exception of Hungary) are Slavic-speaking countries. In contrast, the language of Romania is a Romance language—that is, it is derived from the ancient Latin of the Romans, as are the French, Italian, and Spanish languages. This shows the great resilience of the Romanian people and their culture.

Survival: Given its strategic position in the Balkan Peninsula and the many invasions of the country over the centuries—including periods of occupation by the Ottoman Turks from the thirteenth century until 1878—this land has fought hard for its right to exist. On the other hand, of course, the language and culture also reflect long contact with the Slavs, Turks, and others, making Romania a fertile crossroads of peoples.

Aesthetic Features: Romanian culture is rich and active. There are numerous dance and folklore groups from all its provinces that regularly win prizes in international competition. The costumes, dances, and songs are sumptuous; typical Romanians can often be heard singing a large repertoire of traditional songs at parties and anniversaries. Like the Ukrainians and Poles, the Romanians carry on the tradition of the *pasanka* or ornately decorated eggs for Easter celebrations. Some areas of Romania also continue the centuries-old fabrication of delicate lace tablecloths, napkins, and dress designs.

Architecturally speaking, Romania can boast an extraordinary number of beautifully preserved medieval historic city centers, castles, churches, and monasteries—particularly in the area of Sighisoara and Brashov in the center of the country. Icons adorn church walls; tapestries and oriental rugs decorate walls and flagstone floors.

Romanian Character and Pride: Romanians are often described as warm and friendly, thus making conversation with them quite easy. They speak with pride of their historic land.

Pacala (Romania)—
Follow-Up Information and Activities

A LOOK AT CULTURES

The story *Pacala* and the accompanying information offered insight into Romania's culture. If you were asked to provide a one-page description of your own culture, identify at least ten major points you would like to make.

_____

_____

_____

_____

_____

_____

_____

_____

_____

_____

_____

If you were asked to *contrast* your culture with Romania, what would be the major points of this contrast?

_____

_____

_____

_____

_____

_____

_____

_____

_____

_____

_____

_____

_____

Pacala (Romania)—
Wrap-Up Activity

GAME SHOW FUN

To leaders of the game show activities: Use the following questions in your favorite game show format. (See page xv for activity suggestions.) These questions may be shown on an overhead projector or prepared as separate cards. For an easier round of questions, include the four choices of answers. For a more challenging experience, use only the question stem (without the choices of answers). The questions relate to the story content only. (Answers appear on page xvi.) Additional questions may be prepared from the specific cultural information provided in this section or discovered by the involved learners.

Questions from the Story Content

1. When the popa tried to anger Pacala by sending him to work without anything to eat, what was Pacala's strategy?

    A.   He simply chose to fast for that day.

    B.   He used his cleverness to prepare food from available resources around him.

    C.   He sold the popa's grain and bought himself a meal.

    D.   He begged food from a neighbor.

2. When the popa gave Pacala bread and cheese for his meal but ordered him to return them at the end of the day, how did Pacala manage to gain nourishment for the day?

    A.   He sold them both and used the money to buy twice the amount of a less expensive bread and cheese. He ate half and returned the other half to the popa.

    B.   He returned them both, but not before he secretly spat upon them.

    C.   He pled with the popa's wife to give him enough nourishment to sustain him throughout the day.

    D.   He bored a hole in each and scraped out the innards, leaving the original outer shape.

3. How did Pacala's magical flute enrage the popa?

    A. It caused the popa's wife to dance until she fell from the attic step and broke several bones.

    B. It caused the popa's sheep to dance until they died from exhaustion.

    C. The music from the flute was so soothing that it put the popa in a better mood than he desired.

    D. It caused the popa to become extremely jealous of Pacala's musical talents, and he broke Pacala's flute.

4. If the popa had ordered Pacala to build a barn in one day, how might Pacala have responded?

    A. He might have complained that such a task couldn't be accomplished in one day.

    B. He would probably have demanded a staff of workers to help him with the task.

    C. He would have become enraged but would have begun the project.

    D. By the end of the day he might have built a miniature barn, thus accomplishing the task.

5. Why didn't Pacala drown the popa's son when he was told to do so?

    A. He wanted to kill the son in a manner more violent than drowning.

    B. He had no quarrel with the son and didn't want to harm him.

    C. He and the son were good friends, and both hated the father.

    D. The son was much stronger than Pacala; therefore, the son escaped.

6. Pacala was primarily presented as a puckish and but ultimately compassionate character in this story. Why did he commit the violent act of cutting off the tip of the popa's nose?

    A. He felt it was the only way to teach the popa a lesson he needed to learn.

    B. The villagers all wanted to see the popa's nose chopped off.

    C. Pacala's secret passion was chopping off noses.

    D. The popa's nose had grown too long, and it needed a cosmetic "trim."

Questions About Vocabulary Terms from the Story

7.   What is the occupation of someone called a popa?

   A.   A minister

   B.   A prison warden

   C.   An executioner

   D.   A cook

8.   Pacala could be described as being puckish. What does puckish mean?

   A.   Wild

   B.   Wonderful

   C.   Whimsical

   D.   White-livered

9.   The popa in this story acted in a haughty manner. How does someone act who is haughty?

   A.   Delightfully presidential

   B.   Delicately presumptuous

   C.   Dolefully perceptive

   D.   Disdainfully proud

Questions About the Pacala Character

10.   What particular character and genre does Pacala represent?

   A.   An antagonist in Romanian mystery stories

   B.   A popular hero in Romanian folklore

   C.   A religious figure in Romanian novels

   D.   A protagonist in Romanian drama

11.   Why is Pacala an admired character in Romania?

    A.   He took a stand against injustice.

    B.   He conquered the popas in his region.

    C.   He fought in many Romanian battles.

    D.   He could survive the fiercest war difficulties.

12.   What was the "Pacala Cycle"?

    A.   A vehicle having only one wheel that was often used in Romanian carnivals

    B.   A one-year period of rule by a Romanian king

    C.   A series of relatively short, humorous Romanian stories

    D.   The circular area in the Romanian churches where commoners stood to pray

13.   What type of character was Pacala in this story?

    A.   Trickster

    B.   Villain

    C.   Underdog

    D.   Heroine

Questions About Romania

14.   What is the largest land region (province) in Romania?

    A.   Muldovia

    B.   Bukovina

    C.   Dobruja

    D.   Transylvania

15. What character do most people think of when someone mentions Transylvania?

   A.   Julius Caesar (a ruler in ancient Rome)

   B.   Sam yada Cannarozzi (a Yugoslavian storyteller)

   C.   Turk Ottama (a fabricated infracaninophile)

   D.   Dracula (Vlad Dracul—a national hero who defended Romania)

Chapter 6

Gilitrutt

*A Folktale
from
Iceland*

About the Contributor

This section was prepared primarily by

Jenni Woodroffe

Jenni Woodroffe (BA, BEd, ALIAA) brings pleasure to young and old with her story-telling. She has been on the story trail through North America, Europe, Asia, New Zealand, and Australia to explore the backgrounds, variants, and connections of the many tales now shared with children and adults. She is a past president of the Storytelling Guild of Australia (WA) and a former tertiary lecturer and teacher librarian. Jenni tells stories and runs workshops to encourage others to tell their story.

Several years ago she visited Iceland and met Dr. Sigrún Klara Hannesdóttir, formerly of the University of Iceland. Thus began her interest in the Icelandic culture and her pursuit of stories from that area. Another colleague who also assisted with the cultural information for *Gilitrutt* was Dr. L. Anne Clyde, Faculty of Social Science, University of Iceland.

Note: This story was adapted from material in the following sources: *Gilitrutt* in *Icelandic Folk and Fairy Tales*, selected and translated by May and Hallberg Hallmundsson, 1987 (Iceland Review Library); and *Elves, Trolls, and Elemental Beings: Icelandic Folktales II*, translated by Alan Boucher, 1977 (Iceland Review Library). These tales were translated from the classic collection of nineteenth-century folklorist Jon Arnason.

Gilitrutt (Iceland)—Cultural Background

THE CULTURAL SIGNIFICANCE OF NAMES

In most cultures an individual's name is very important—not only in the oral tradition but also in myth and religion. Before experiencing this story, think about the following:

Write down all the names by which you are known (including any nicknames or special family names).

_____

What name do you prefer to be called? Why?

_____

Are you named after any special member of the family or another significant person?

_____

What is the significance or meaning of your first name? (If you do not know, ask a resource person for special dictionaries containing such information.)

_____

What is the meaning of your last name?

_____

After learning the meaning of both of your names, are you pleased? Why or why not?

_____

How important is the meaning of names in your culture?

_____

When you encounter someone who just can't remember your name, how does it make you feel?

_____

If you were responsible for assigning a character name for a very special female in a folktale, what would that name be?

_____

What would that name be for a male character?

_____

Gilitrutt

A Folktale from Iceland

Retold by Jenni Woodroffe

There was once a young farmer who lived near the mountain of Eyjafjoll[1] in Iceland. He was rich and prosperous with a large herd of sheep. He was newly married, and he adored his young wife. All day long he worked hard on the farm.

But the young wife did not like to work. She lazily lolled about in their farmhouse,[2] stared out the window, and did almost nothing all day long.

At first the farmer took no notice. He hoped that as the days passed his new bride would become accustomed to the household chores and would manage their home well. He especially looked forward to returning from a day's work to find a hot meat soup waiting for him.[3]

The seasons passed. Lambing and shearing gave way to haymaking. Haymaking gave way to slaughtering. Soon it would be time to house the sheep before the winter snows began.[4]

One evening the farmer brought in an enormous bale of wool. It contained the fleece of every sheep shorn that year.

"Here you are," he said to his wife. "Spin and weave this into cloth.[5] We'll need it for the coming year."

Still the young wife did nothing. Her husband did not like it—not at all.

After the farmer left for work one day, a big ugly old woman appeared at the door.

"Can you spare some alms for a poor old woman?" she asked.

"If you do some work for me first," replied the young woman.

"Maybe I will. Maybe I won't. What do you want done?" the old woman asked.

"Can you spin and weave all this wool into cloth for me?"

"Give it to me," the old woman said. "I'll be back with the cloth on *Sumardagurinn fyrsti,*[6] the first day of summer. In return, you must tell me my name."

With the heavy bale of wool on her back, the old woman soon disappeared down the path. The days grew shorter and shorter. Snow and ice covered the farm. Still the young wife did nothing.

"How's the weaving coming along?" the farmer asked each day.

"Oh, it's being done," she replied.

As the winter darkness deepened, the young wife began to have doubts. *Will the old woman return? How can I discover her name? Did I give away the entire season's yield? Will we lose the farm because of my foolishness?*

As her fears assailed her, the young woman huddled by the fire. Tears slowly trickled down her face. The farmer begged her to explain her troubles.

"It's the wool. I gave it to an ugly old woman to spin and weave. She'll be back the first day of summer, but I have to know her name in order to get the cloth." Her tears continued to fall.

The farmer was dismayed as he looked at his young and foolish bride. Had she been trapped by an ugly old trollwife?[7] What would become of her?

Now it so happened that he had to go to the foothills. As he was passing a large mound of rocks,[8] he heard a strange noise. He crept closer and closer, and peering through a crack he saw an enormous ugly old woman sitting at a loom, weaving and singing,

Heigh, heigh, and ho, ho,
The fair young wife
Still does not know.
Heigh, heigh, and ho, ho,
Gilitrutt is my name, ho, ho.
Gilitrutt is my name,
Heigh, heigh, and ho, ho!

Over and over he repeated the words he had heard. When he arrived home, he quietly wrote down the name Gilitrutt, but he did not tell his wife.

The last day of winter arrived. By now the young wife was so upset that she could not even get out of bed. She huddled under the bedclothes in the *badstofa* and was so miserable she thought she was going to die.

"Have you discovered the name of the ugly old woman?" her husband asked.

She shook her head. So her husband told her all he had seen and heard.

"Tomorrow is *Sumardagurinn fyrsti,* and your cloth will be ready. See that you are ready too."

"Oh please, husband dear. Stay with me. I'm so afraid."

"Oh no. It was you who made the bargain, and it is you who will see it through." And he left the house.

Before long there was a knock at the door. The young wife opened it. There on the doorstep stood the ugly old troll with a large bundle of finely woven cloth in her arms.

"Now," she said, stepping inside. "Tell me my name."

"Is it Signy?"[9] the young bride asked, trembling with fear.

"It could be that. It could be that. Guess again, mistress," said the old woman.

"Is it Asa?" the young woman tried again.

"It could be that. It could be that. Guess again, mistress," gloated the old woman.

"Is it Gilitrutt?"

The old woman let out a sound like a thunderclap and fell to the floor. The young bride caught the cloth just in time.

Suddenly the old woman gathered herself up, dashed out the door, and was never seen again.

As for the young bride, she was so glad to be freed from the old woman that she soon changed her ways. And from then on she always wove her own wool.[10]

Gilitrutt (Iceland)—
Follow-Up Information and Activities

SPECIFIC CULTURAL NOTES

The information given below refers to the corresponding numbers on the previous pages of the folktale. This is provided for additional insight and cultural information. Use as needed or desired.

Notes

1.   Eyjafjoll (AY-yah-fyerdl) is a mountain close to the ring road between the capital of Iceland (Reykjavik) and Hofn. Skoga Waterfall is nearby.

2.   A typical farmhouse in Iceland at the time of this story was made of stone and turf. The traditional Icelandic farmhouse has a common bed and living room called the *badstofa* (BOD-stow-fuh). The word means "bathroom," and it was originally a sauna. Later it was used for sleeping during the cold winters because the stone oven was used to produce steam for the bath and would keep everything warm. As time went by, the *badstofa* became the hub of the farmhouse where everyone ate, slept, and worked. There were no tables or chairs. The beds were placed along the walls of the building, and each person sat on his or her own bed. Each family member had a personal *askur,* a container similar to a bowl with a lid. Each also had a pocketknife and a spoon made from sheep's horn, often nicely decorated. The housewife would put each individual's rations into his or her own bowl, thus allowing everyone an independent place for eating.

3.   A favorite food at the time of this story was meat soup. This could be quite a luxurious dish made from fresh sheep meat and selected vegetables.

4.   Shearing of the sheep takes place in May so the sheep can exist in comfort without the extra layers of warmth during the warm summer months. Summer is a busy time for haymaking. Because of the long hours of summer sunshine and the heavy rainfall, farmers can raise three crops of hay. Iceland is a land of midnight sun. It is light for twenty-four hours a day in June, but for only about two hours a day during winter.

5.   Most of Iceland is a large plateau. Along the coasts are grassy lowlands where farmers raise sheep. Because summer is such a busy time for haymaking, the farmers keep the wool until the autumn when summer tasks are over and winter is approaching.

6.   *Sumardagurinn fyrsti* (SUE-mar-dog-your-in FEARST-ee) is the first day of summer (*sumar* means summer; *dagur* means day; *inn* is the definite article "the"—attached to the word itself; and *fyrsti* means first.) It occurs on a Thursday between the nineteenth and the twenty-sixth of April. It is a celebration that dates back to Iceland's medieval calendar, and it is still a public holiday. It is the first day of a month called Harpa in the old Icelandic calendar—a month that marked the time when the day began to be noticeably longer than the night. It was a major festival (often celebrated with more enthusiasm than Christmas) when children were given "summer gifts." The greeting *Gleðilegt sumar* (meaning happy summer, pronounced *GLEE-thil-legt SUE-mar*) is still heard today.

7.   The size of the trolls relates to the mountains and volcanoes of Iceland's land of frost and fire. The trolls are ugly, and some are as big as the mountains of Iceland (lying just below the Arctic Circle in the North Atlantic Ocean) where earthquakes, glaciers, and geysers abound. They are different from the *huldufolk* (HULLED-uh-folk, the common name for elves), which means "hidden people."

8.   Because of the volcanic nature of the land, rock formations are everywhere. They are grey and bleak. Legend has it that any troll who sees the sun is turned into stone, thus adding to these formations. Trolls live underground, where the rushing and hissing sounds of the geysers add to the already eerie visual environment.

9.   In Iceland, people are properly called by their first names, which they are given at baptism. Their last name is their father's own name (or given name), followed by *dóttir* for females, and *son* for males. Therefore, if Signy's father had been Olaf, she would have been known as Signy Olafsdóttir.

10.   One main theme of this story is the importance of work. It is deeply rooted in a society in which there has never been an aristocracy, in which there were no really rich people, in which all people had to work if they were to survive the long winters and the harsh climate. Even children had their work, and their work was valuable. Any person not pulling his or her weight was a strain on the others, even in the largest family household, and that person's laziness could make it difficult for the others to survive. Characteristics that are important for the survival of all are reinforced throughout this story. The message is that those who don't work will expose themselves and others to difficulties and loss. Another thought is that those who don't go to church and don't give gifts to the people who work on their land might be taken away by the *jólasveinar*! (See next page for a related activity.)

Pronunciation Information: The suggested pronunciations of some Icelandic words may appear to be unusual. There are several letters or symbols that may have different sound-letter associations from those of your native tongue. For example, the symbol ð in Icelandic words generally represents the sound of *th-*, as in the word *that*. Another interesting feature in Icelandic pronunciations is that the first syllable of polysyllabic words is always stressed. A possible added cultural experience for listeners is to listen for other pronunciation differences of native speakers from other regions of the world.

Gilitrutt (Iceland)—
Follow-Up Information and Activities

THE POWER OF NAMES IN OTHER CULTURES

Knowledge of names is often equated with power in many cultures. In some cultures a person's name is so private that few individuals beyond the family know it. In the story *Gilitrutt*, knowing someone's name was important. It gave the farmer's wife the power to regain possession of her goods.

There are folktales in other cultures that are based on the widespread belief that the knowledge of the name of a hostile person or thing gives power. You may be familiar with the story *Rumplestiltskin* (recorded by Jacob and Wilhelm Grimm in Germany) that has a similar motif to *Gilitrutt*. Other stories with similar plots are *Tom-Tit-Tot* (from Suffolk, England), *Habetrot and Scatlie Mab* (from Yorkshire, England), and *Whuppity Stourie* (from Scotland). Find one of these stories and respond to the following:

Title and culture of selected story: _____

Why did the young woman in your selected story have to find the name of the mysterious person? (How does this relate to the culture reflected in the story?)_____

_____

_____

How was the name of the mysterious person discovered? (Was this discovery of any cultural significance?) _____

_____

_____

What happened to the mysterious person when the name was discovered?_____

_____

_____

How did the ending differ from *Gilitrutt*? _____

_____

_____

_____

Identify at least three other cultural differences between your selected story and *Gilitrutt*.

_____

_____

_____

Gilitrutt (Iceland)—
Follow-Up Information and Activities

CULTURAL EXTENSIONS: ICELANDIC HOLIDAYS

Holidays are celebrated in many ways in various cultures. Have fun with the following holiday thoughts.

What is your favorite holiday in your culture? Identify one favorite food that you associate with that holiday. Is that food generally eaten only during that holiday period? What kind of special preparation is needed for this favorite holiday food? Compare your thoughts with the Icelandic celebrations explained at the right.

Answer: _____
_____
_____
_____
_____
_____

Christmas is an important celebration in Iceland. A special kind of bread is eaten with the Christmas meal. It is called *laufabrauð* (leaf-bread, LURV-uh-brerth). This is flat, unleavened bread that is deep fried. A special cutter made of copper is used to make a basic pattern. The cut sections are woven by hand to make patterns that look like the leaves for which the bread is named. Making the *laufabrauð* is a family occasion when the extended family members gather for the day. Adults make the pastry mixture and roll it out, cutting circles about six to eight inches in diameter. Children make the patterns in the bread. Each generation teaches the tradition to the next one. Some people choose a pattern based on the first letter of their name, and everyone seems to have a favorite pattern. The older women cook the bread in a manner that requires standing for long hours over a cauldron of hot fat. Some families have special plates on which the *laufabrauð* is served. These plates are handed down from one generation to the next.

Is there a favorite holiday character in your culture? Identify this character and explain his or her role in the corresponding holiday season. Compare your thoughts with the Icelandic characters explained here.

Answer: _____
_____
_____
_____
_____
_____
_____
_____
_____
_____
_____
_____
_____

Instead of Santa Claus, Iceland has its own "Christmas Men" known as *jólasveinar* (JUH-loss-vain-ar). There are thirteen *jólasveinar* who arrive from the mountains one at a time on each of the thirteen days before Christmas and then depart one by one on the thirteen days after Christmas. They are not pleasant or jolly, and they are not gift bringers. They are tricksters, and their names indicate their activities (e.g., Window-peeper, Sausage-snatcher, Candle-stealer, etc.). They are blamed for everything that goes wrong during the Christmas season, and they are used to threaten children who misbehave. If anyone stayed home from church on Christmas Eve, the *jólasveinar* would come and carry him or her away. They would also play tricks on farmers who did not give gifts to the people who had worked for them.

Gilitrutt (Iceland)—
Wrap-Up Activity

GAME SHOW FUN

To leaders of the game show activities: Use the following questions in your favorite game show format. (See page xv for activity suggestions.) These questions may be shown on an overhead projector or prepared as separate cards. For an easier round of questions, include the four choices of answers. For a more challenging experience, use only the question stem (without the choices of answers). The questions relate to the story content only. (Answers appear on page xvi.) Additional questions may be prepared from the specific cultural information provided in this section or discovered by the involved learners.

Questions from the Story Content

1. What story in folklore has a plot that resembles the one in *Gilitrutt*?

    A. Cinderella

    B. Goldilocks and the Three Bears

    C. Snow White and the Seven Dwarfs

    D. Rumplestiltskin

2. What did the housewife in this story seem to be suffering from?

    A. Exhaustion from being overworked

    B. Lack of motivation

    C. Depression

    D. Immobility

3. In what way did the young farmer want his wife to change?

    A. He wanted her to do the household chores.

    B. He wanted her to be a good weaver.

    C. He wanted her to be more beautiful.

    D. He wanted her to work outside in the fields with him.

4. What did Gilitrutt do immediately after the wife guessed her name?

   A. She demanded their firstborn child.

   B. She cast a spell on the young wife.

   C. She disappeared in a clap of thunder.

   D. She changed her name to "Signy" so this episode wouldn't repeat itself.

5. What lesson did the housewife learn from this experience?

   A. That she should get others to weave her wool

   B. That her husband can step in and solve any problem she encounters in the future

   C. That she can depend on trollwives to do her chores for her

   D. That she should take responsibility for what is expected of her

Questions About Vocabulary Terms from the Story

6. The young farmer hoped that hot meat soup would be waiting for him at the end of his working day. What are some of the ingredients of meat soup?

   A. Sheep meat and vegetables

   B. Rice and wool

   C. Troll meat and spices

   D. Liver and gizzards from Gilitrutts

7. When Gilitrutt first appeared at the young wife's door, she asked if the wife could spare some alms. What are alms?

   A. Bales of hay, wool, and so forth that can be made into fabrics

   B. Special assistance with carrying heavy burdens (such as slaughtered sheep)

   C. Small, circular, green fruits (similar to olives) that produce valued cooking oils

   D. Something (such as money or food) given freely to relieve the poor

8. Gilitrutt promised to return the spun cloth on *Sumardagurinn fyrsti*. When would that be?

    A. The first day of the new year

    B. Any time after the wife had given birth to her first child

    C. The first summer of a newly married couple's life together

    D. The first day of summer

9. Gilitrutt carried a heavy bale of wool on her back. What is a bale?

    A. A backpack designed to keep loose and lightweight items from blowing away in the wind

    B. A barrel-shaped container that won't easily break

    C. A large closely pressed package of goods

    D. A crush-proof, balloon-shaped pouch

10. When the young wife was worried about what she had done, she huddled in the *badstofa*. What is a *badstofa*?

    A. A waiting area for sick or distressed individuals

    B. An oversized, stuffed couch

    C. A common bedroom and living room

    D. A place where bad people are sent as punishment for their misdeeds

Questions About Iceland and Its Culture

11. Farmers in Iceland shear their sheep during the month of May. Why is that month selected?

    A. The major religions in Iceland dictate that the sheep be sheared before *Sumardagurinn fyrsti.*

    B. After the month of May, the sheep will be experiencing a long hibernation period; therefore the wool must be taken in May so their sleep will not be disturbed.

    C. Summer is approaching and the sheep will be more comfortable without the extra layers of warmth.

    D. The period of heavy rainfall has just ended, and the sheep-shearing tasks are considerably easier during a dry season.

12. Why do Icelandic farmers save the wool from their sheep until autumn to process?

    A. They do not handle the wool during the summer season because hay-making chores take all their work time.

    B. The wool needs to remain in a waterproof shed so it can dry out before it is processed.

    C. During the summer months the farmers use the unprocessed wool for insulation in their homes.

    D. The sheep need to stay close to their sheared wool for a period of time so they will not experience shock from losing it.

13. Why is knowledge of a character's name an important element in this story?

    A. Icelanders would sometimes change their name if they were in trouble or deeply in debt, so knowing someone's current name could be valuable.

    B. In the Icelandic culture, knowing someone's name was equated with power.

    C. A person's name was always associated with the legendary trolls, and knowledge of the name could help avoid disaster.

    D. If a person's name rhymed with a famous church in the area, then it was good luck to develop a friendship with him or her.

14. Unlike the typical Santa Claus known in many American cultures, Iceland has "Christmas Men." Describe these men.

   A. They are not pleasant or jolly.

   B. They are not gift bringers.

   C. They are tricksters.

   D. All of the above

15. The story's main theme emphasizes a deeply rooted principle of Icelandic society. What is this theme?

   A. Protecting the family name is the most important personal goal one should have.

   B. The sheep-shearing and haymaking schedules must be honored and respected at all times.

   C. A person must live a very cautious life to avoid being turned into stone.

   D. Hard work is important for individuals and families to survive.

Chapter 7

Nasreddin Odjah's Clothes

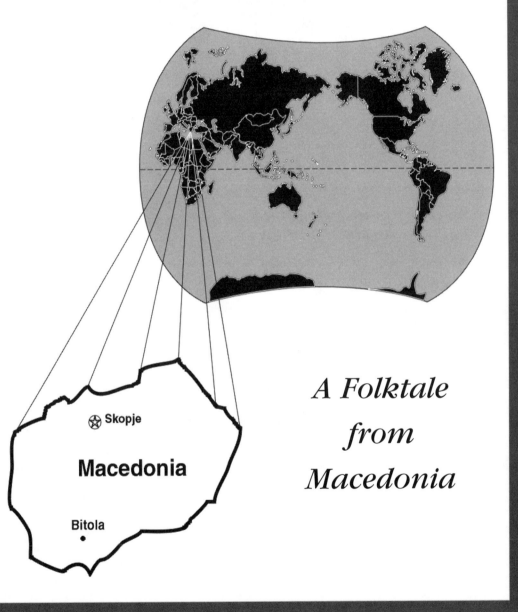

Skopje

Macedonia

Bitola

A Folktale

from

Macedonia

About the Contributor

This section was prepared primarily by

Steven Kardaleff

Steven Kardaleff brings *Nasreddin Odjah's Clothes* to you from the Slavic Macedonian oral tradition. The story came to Macedonia with the invading Turkish armies of the Ottoman Empire sometime after 1389. The rebellion against the Turkish occupation of Macedonia (for more than five hundred years) began in 1903, the birth year of Steven's father, whose birth certificate was written in Turkish. Both of Steven's parents were born in Bitola, Macedonia. The Turks learned that his grandfather was involved with the *komiti* (koh-MEE-tee)—rebels against the Ottomans. His grandfather's flight from Turkish justice brought Steven's father to the United States as a preschool boy. The father of Steven's mother was an Eastern Orthodox priest who died while serving as a chaplain in World War I. She came to America as a young woman shortly before World War II. Steven's parents met and married in the United States.

He chose Bitola as the setting for the story because his mother learned the story as she was growing up there. He learned *Nasreddin Odjah's Clothes* from her when he was six years old, and it is the first tale he told to a story-listening audience.

Currently Steven lives in Lawton, Oklahoma. He is a businessman, university teacher, freelance storyteller, and former executive director of the National Storytelling Network.

Nasreddin Odjah's Clothes (Macedonia)— Cultural Background

DON'T "CLOTHES" THE DOOR

Before experiencing the story *Nasreddin Odjah's Clothes,* think about the meaning of the following proverb: *Never judge a book by its cover.*

What do you think this proverb means? Have you ever judged people by how they appeared rather than by their inner qualities? What emphasis does your culture place on outward appearances? What emphasis do you feel *should* be placed on outward appearances? Think about these factors as you read or hear the story about Nasreddin.

 ## HISTORICAL BACKGROUND

Nasreddin and Timur: Turkey was conquered by the Mongol emperor Timur the Lame (also known as Tamberlane) early in the fourteenth century. Turkish serfs suffered for many decades under Timur's stern rule. One serf who challenged Timur was Nasreddin Odjah. Brief stories chronicle meetings between these two men. Nasreddin was always apprehensive about these encounters because Timur's unpredictable wrath was legendary. But the Mongol conqueror never harmed Nasreddin; instead, he delighted in Nasreddin's nimbleness of mind, dexterity in speech, and courage to respond boldly in the face of certain danger.

Nasreddin to the Rescue: Because he could easily sidestep Timur's loaded questions and turn them into witty rejoinders, Nasreddin became the folk hero of other Turkish serfs. They often told each other stories of how Nasreddin had outwitted Timur. Each retelling of these encounters cheered up the serfs' downtrodden hearts. In this way the Turks never allowed their Mongol oppressors to vanquish their spirit.

The Ottoman Empire: When Timur finally died, the Turks drove out the Mongols and regained their freedom. Ottoman armies spread across northern Africa, and in 1389 Turkish soldiers invaded and conquered southeastern Europe (including Macedonia). The invaders and the Macedonian Slavs spoke different languages. They also practiced different religions. The Turks were followers of Islam, and the Slavs were Eastern Orthodox Christians. Because the Turks did not impose their culture on the people they subjugated, the Slavs were free to speak their own language and attend their own schools and churches.

New Concerns: The Turkish Sultan, chief sovereign of the Ottoman Empire, simplified ruling his subjects to just two concerns: one was an imposition, the other a demand. The imposition was straightforward: Turkish would be the official language of governance. The demand was even simpler: absolute obedience. That obedience began with the realization that the Sultan *owned everything* in a conquered land: crops, fields, livestock, buildings, and the people, too. (Steven Kardaleff's father was the last of the family to be born as chattel of the Sultan.)

The Functioning of the Bey: A Bey was a Turkish gentleman of importance, the Sultan's representative and administrator in a region of the Ottoman Empire. The Sultan would allot a Bey in his service a portion of the conquered land. The Bey was master of that district and all things in it. It was the Bey's duty to govern and work that area for the Sultan's (and his own) profit. He kept his position by demonstrating his ability to execute that duty. All officials under the Bey kept their jobs in a like manner.

The Aggressive Protest: Life was difficult for the serfs. They were overworked and underfed. But things can always get worse. At times the profit generated from a region was the result of extreme misery. For example, if the grain harvest was less than expected, local overseers would make the serfs surrender that portion of the grain allotted to them for survival through the winter. It was under such extreme circumstances of near starvation that Macedonian serfs employed stealth to survive. They turned in the grain to the overseer, who inventoried it as they stored it in the Bey's warehouse. At night they would steal back their grain. [1]

Nasreddin as a Secondhand Hero of the Oppressed Macedonians: It is ironic that Nasreddin Odjah's wiliness relieved the defiant Macedonian serfs. His stories originated among the Turks, but later lifted and upheld the spirits of the oppressed Slavs as they struggled to survive exploitation by their Ottoman masters. The Slavic serfs did not embrace other Middle Eastern heroes (like Sinbad or Aladdin) because they had their own folk heroes who struck out on bold adventures (such as Marko, Silyan, and Prince Ivan). What they needed was a hero with the common man's fears, weaknesses, and hopes—plus a quick agile mind that could turn misfortune into benefit. Nasreddin was such a character, so they adopted him as the folk hero of their spirit. His place in the Slavic cultural folklore is unique, not because of his Near Eastern name and Turkish honorific title, but because he nurtured nonaggressive protest with dignity. In fact, the irony of his being Turkish only served to increase the deception and extend the humor.

PRONUNCIATION GUIDE

The words that follow are used in this story. No standard diacritical or pronunciation system is used; instead, real or pseudo-words are offered as pronunciation aids. Stressed syllables are printed in SOLID CAPS, as other contributors have used in this book.

Nasreddin (nas-ruh-DEEN)   *Odjah* (OH-juh)

Bitola (bi-TOLL-uh)   *Koran* (kuh-RAN)

Effendi (eh-FEND-ee) (means "Sir")   *Bey* (BAY)

Ak-hisar (ak-hi-SAR)   *baklava* (BOCK-luh-vah)

[1] **A Cross-Cultural Side Note:** This type of survival tactic reveals itself in folklore of other cultures that were characterized by abusive masters. In Roger D. Abrahams's *Afro-American Folktales,* a slave became an expert in stealing pigs because his master would give him no meat. The tales of this type of encounter are referred to as "Old John and Massa" stories. A point for cultural discussions could include the survival tactics employed by mistreated workers.

Nasreddin Odjah's Clothes

A Folktale from Macedonia

Retold by Steven Kardaleff

A long time ago a certain man lived in Bitola, Macedonia, east of Italy across the pale blue Adriatic Sea. The man was neither rich nor poor, arrogant nor meek, faultless nor corrupt. His name was Nasreddin, and he was an odjah—a man educated in the teaching of the Koran who could earn his living by serving as a teacher, a judge, or a preacher. The townsfolk respected him for his wisdom about the ways of people.

One day Nasreddin decided to call on a sick friend who lived in a small mountain village on the outskirts of Bitola. He dressed for traveling, put on his odjah's turban, and left town. He had a pleasant visit. As the sun began to set behind the mountain, Nasreddin started walking home, eager for his supper. His sick friend hadn't fed him. (How could he? He was sick!)

When he saw the first house near the town, his empty stomach growled, and he suddenly remembered he was invited to attend a wedding feast that evening. "It's late already!" he thought. "To be on time, I must go directly from here. They'll be glad to see me." So he abandoned his homeward trek, brushed the road dust from his clothes, and made straight for the wedding supper.

When he arrived, he found a throng of guests surrounding the one entrance through the high walls enclosing the residence. Shortly two servants emerged, lined up the guests, and began admitting them in an orderly fashion. Nasreddin noticed the servants had placed all the better-dressed people at the front of the line, and they put him at the very end. Not only that, but as new guests arrived, they were always put ahead of him.

Nasreddin left for home where he dressed in his finest clothes: red goatskin slippers with turned-up toes, baggy flannel pants, paisley cummerbund, linen shirt, soft cashmere cloak with long sleeves, and his odjah's turban with fine cloth wrapped around the red felt crown. Then he returned to the feast.

When the other guests saw him this time, they shouted his name, shook his hand, and patted him on the back as the servants quickly took him inside. They ushered him by the serving tables loaded with wine, breads, and baklava. Finally they seated him in a place of honor next to the head table. Nasreddin nodded to the wedding party and the other guests. They smiled back.

A large tray of roasted meat and a big bowl of steaming gravy were placed before the odjah. He drew in a deep breath, closed his eyes, enjoyed the meat's savory smell, and said a prayer to Allah. Having given thanks, he reached over, took a piece of meat and stuffed it into his shirt. He poked the next piece into his cummerbund.

Then he jammed one into each pocket of his pants. All eyes were on Nasreddin as he gathered the long sleeves of his cloak and soaked them in the bowl of hot gravy.

A stunned guest jumped to his feet and demanded, "*Effendi!* What is the meaning of your outrageous behavior?"

"Well," said Nasreddin Odjah, "when you find yourself in a place where clothes are more welcomed than the person wearing them, you must feed the clothes first and the person afterward!"

Nasreddin Odjah's Clothes (Macedonia)—
Follow-Up Information and Activities

WHO WAS NASREDDIN ODJAH?

What Is an Odjah? The word *odjah* is a title, not a name. In the Slavic cultures, this title follows the person's name, in contrast to the positioning of titles in many other cultures. An odjah was a highly respected person in the days of the Ottoman Empire (1300–1919). He had a rare possession that the Ottomans highly prized: a formal education. Besides being taught to read and write, he was tutored in the teachings of the Koran. As an odjah, he could seek employment as a teacher, a judge (because Islamic law was based on the teaching of the Koran), or a preacher. The odjah wore a unique turban. The cloth was not applied directly to the head, but wrapped around a felt crown. This made it easy to find him in public places when someone needed his services. For example, an illiterate person who received a letter could seek an odjah, who was obliged to read it for free but could charge a modest fee if a written reply were requested.

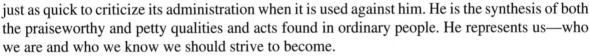

What Did Nasreddin Odjah Look Like? Whenever Nasreddin is mentioned, folks imagine a slightly overweight, white-bearded man wearing slippers, baggy flannel pants, a collarless linen shirt, sleeveless robe, and an odjah's turban.

What Kind of Person Was He? Nasreddin represents the noblest and pettiest aspects of all humankind. In his stories he is often extremely wise, but just as often foolish or pigheaded; alternately clever and utterly stupid; altruistic, but secretly dreaming of riches to satisfy his own fancy; guided by common sense or given to whimsy; quick to obey the law, but just as quick to criticize its administration when it is used against him. He is the synthesis of both the praiseworthy and petty qualities and acts found in ordinary people. He represents us—who we are and who we know we should strive to become.

Did He Really Exist? It is not known for certain that this odjah, Nasreddin, ever really existed. New stories, anecdotes, and jests have been attributed to him for more than two centuries after his supposed death, many in locales too distant for him to have visited in his lifetime. Whether he ever lived or not, he did exist and still does exist in story. Every year from July 5 through 10 the Turkish government's Department of Tourism sponsors an International Nasreddin Odjah Festival to honor him in Ak-hisar, Turkey.

Does He Have a Grave? A grave said to be Nasreddin's is in Ak-hisar. Perhaps the most eloquent of all statements about this unusual man is his gravesite. In front of the ordinary grave is an amply padlocked, waist-high iron gate. But there is no wall or fence to this locked entrance.

What Kinds of Stories Exist About Him? Because Nasreddin Odjah stories deal with excesses, they are humorous rather than preachy. This story genre is called *swank,* a technical German folklore term. This form of story is also called a numskull, noodlehead, nitwit, or trickster tale in the literature dealing with folktale scholarship.

Nasreddin Odjah's Clothes (Macedonia)—
Follow-Up Information and Activities

OUTWARD APPEARANCES

How do you think Nasreddin felt about the proverb "Never judge a book by its cover"?

_____

_____

Other cultures have proverbs with similar meanings. The following are some ways that different cultures have expressed this same important message:

Appearances are deceiving.
—the moral of Aesop's fable *"The Wolf in Sheep's Clothing"*

Beware of all enterprises that require new clothes.
—from Henry David Thoreau in *Walden*

Clothes make the man.
—a paraphrase from Shakespeare's *Hamlet*

. . . every true man's apparel fits a thief . . .
—from Shakespeare's *Measure for Measure*

How do people in your culture feel about outward appearances?

_____

_____

_____

Describe or draw how you think Nasreddin Odjah's traveling clothes would be different from the fine clothes he put on later.

_____

_____

_____

Is it socially acceptable today in your culture to wear any kind of clothing to every kind of event? Which events? Why or why not?

_____

_____

_____

Nasreddin Odjah's Clothes (Macedonia)— Follow-Up Information and Activities

BEYOND THE STORY: MACEDONIAN MARRIAGES

During the time of the story, young men and women could not pledge to marry each other in Macedonia. Marriages were arranged between families once they agreed on the terms of the marriage contract. Brokers called *strojnitsi* (STROY-neet-see), or matchmakers, negotiated betrothals. The terms depended on the family's position in the community and the future bride's and groom's respective age, beauty, intelligence, personal wealth or dowry, and industriousness. (For example, older men needed to have more wealth, and less attractive women needed to have larger dowries.) If both families trusted a single broker, the arrangements were made quickly. If not, each family had its own matchmaker, and the negotiations became quite lengthy. The father and mother instructed the matchmaker about their terms and rarely consulted the prospective bride and groom. Furthermore, it was not unusual for a bride and groom to have never met until the day their engagement was announced.

The Dowry. The bride's dowry consisted of all of her accumulated belongings, including the personal property her parents had given her. Little girls were taught needlework before they started school. Even at this early age, some of the items they made went into their hope chests. The following were the actual items in the dowry of Domnicka Mateeva (Steven Kardaleff's grandmother):

1 vineyard
1 silk dress for a bride
2 more dresses, woolen and muslin
1 all-wool dress
1 satin robe
40 men's shirts (silk and cotton) for gifts
4 petticoats (3 percale and 1 muslin)
3 other petticoats
15 different colored cotton head scarves
1 white calico blouse
2 3-inch thick goat-wool mattresses
2 small feather pillows
1 heavy woolen blanket
2 pairs of gold earrings
2 gold bracelets

12½ Turkish lira (and ½ lira more)
2 other silk dresses
1 calico dress
1 quilted robe
2 fur and cloth coats
40 colorful pairs of stockings (for gifts)
2 woolen petticoats
12 colored silk head scarves
2 white fancy eyelet blouses
1 black silk blouse
4 large feather pillows
1 satin/cotton quilt
1 coverlet
1 brooch

Your Challenge. Girls: On separate paper prepare a list of the items that could be in your dowry. **Boys:** Make a list of items you hope would be in your bride's dowry. **Both:** Contrast the value of these material items with other qualities you might have to offer a potential spouse.

Nasreddin Odjah's Clothes (Macedonia)— Follow-Up Information and Activities

MORE ABOUT MACEDONIAN CULTURE

The story about Nasreddin provided a view of one of the folk heroes of Macedonia. There are many facets of Macedonian culture that are likely different from yours. The following are some cultural facts:

- A favorite dessert in Macedonia is **baklava**. Inquire at your local bakery or find a recipe for baklava to see how it tastes.
  Fun for Listeners: How does baklava compare with your favorite dessert?

- **High-Walled Residences.** High, windowless walls around residences were common in regions plagued by continual war. This defensive architecture also allowed the Macedonian townsmen to screen their womenfolk (especially teenaged daughters) from public view.
  Listener Challenge: Contrast this with the architecture of your own residence.

- **Eastern Orthodox Icons.** Icons are religious images painted on wooden panels in a flat two-dimensional style. This style of painting closely resembles mosaic representations of holy figures and scenes. The eleventh-century schism between Rome and Constantinople resulted in two factions of apostolic Christianity: Roman Catholicism in the West and Eastern Orthodoxy in the East. In response to differences raised during the schism, the Orthodox Christians forswore the use of statuary representations of holy figures and replaced statues in their churches with painted icons.

- **Saints Cyril and Methodius, Old Church Slavonic, Macedonian Language.** The Cyrillic alphabet was invented early in the ninth century by two brothers, Cyril and Methodius, who became monks and Greek scholars. This alphabet described the spoken language of Macedonia. They used Greek letters to represent phonemes found in both Greek and Macedonian, then they invented symbols for the sounds found only in Macedonian. Clergymen of Eastern Orthodoxy adopted the Cyrillic alphabet to record their religious rites. In this way Eastern Orthodox practices became uniform throughout the Slavic-speaking cultures. Soon individual Slavic cultures developed their own written languages using the Cyrillic alphabet. Ironically, this did not happen in Macedonia because it was constantly conquered by stronger cultures that forced the Macedonians to learn their conquerors' written languages. From 1900–1950, any Macedonians living in Bitola who sought an education had to attend a school taught in one of the following languages: Bulgarian, Serbian, Greek, French, German, or Turkish. Macedonian did not become a written language until 1948. Macedonian schools began using this language in the mid-1950s.
  Listener Challenge: Investigate the origin of your own alphabet.

Nasreddin Odjah's Clothes (Macedonia)— Wrap-Up Activity

GAME SHOW FUN

To leaders of the game show activities: Use the following questions below in your favorite game show format. (See page xv for activity suggestions.) These questions may be shown on an overhead projector or prepared as separate cards. For an easier round of questions, include the four choices of answers. For a more challenging experience, use only the question stem (without the choices of answers). The questions relate to the story content only. (Answers appear on page xvi.) Additional questions may be prepared from the specific cultural information provided in this section or discovered by the involved learners.

Questions from the Story Content

1. What did the guests have to do to get to the front of the line at the wedding supper in this story?

    A. Arrive early.

    B. Have an aggressive attitude.

    C. Bring gifts for the bride and groom.

    D. Wear fine clothes.

2. Why was Nasreddin so informally dressed and dusty when he first arrived at the wedding supper?

    A. He had forgotten to inquire in advance about the attire, so he ambled in wearing his work clothes.

    B. He had been traveling by foot from a nearby mountain village and didn't take the time to change his clothes.

    C. He had been working in a neighbor's garden for several hours prior to the wedding.

    D. Street robbers had just mugged him and left him in a muddy ditch.

3. Why did Nasreddin Odjah put food in and on his clothes at the wedding feast?

    A. To steal the attention away from the bride and groom

    B. To have food to take back to his sick friend

    C. To make the point that his clothes had been honored more than he himself had been

    D. To entertain the wedding guests in a humorous manner

4. If Nasreddin Odjah were going to a similar wedding feast today, how might he choose to dress?

    A. In shabby clothes—just to see how he would be respected

    B. In his finest clothes—to prove to people that he owned several expensive garments

    C. In clothes that contained many pockets—so he could load them up with food

    D. In a costume so unusual that no one could possibly recognize him

5. Identify a proverb or wise old saying that parallels the lesson of this folktale.

    A. A fool and his food are soon parted.

    B. You can catch more flies with honey than with vinegar.

    C. You can lead a horse to water, but you can't make it drink.

    D. Don't judge a book by its cover.

Questions About the Nasreddin Odjah Character

6. When the word *odjah* follows a person's name in Slavic cultures, what does it signify?

    A. A person who is highly respected and educated

    B. One who owes a great deal of money to the government

    C. A very religious and devout traveler

    D. Someone who is highly skilled in culinary talents

7. Describe Nasreddin's intellectual characteristics.

    A.   He was both wise and foolish.

    B.   He was both brilliantly clever and utterly stupid.

    C.   He was both law abiding and critical of governing bodies.

    D.   He was all of the above.

8. Did Nasreddin Odjah ever really exist?

    A.   He actually lived from 1364–1447 during the days of the Ottoman Empire.

    B.   He exists through stories such as this one.

    C.   Records of his birth were destroyed, but several old Bibles have his name recorded in them along with many of his other family members.

    D.   Similar to the case of Zorro, a group of people masqueraded as Nasreddin over the years; therefore, his identity is unknown.

9. How did the Macedonian serfs feel about Nasreddin Odjah?

    A.   He was viewed as an aggressive protestor without dignity.

    B.   He was perceived as someone comparable to the court jester.

    C.   He was their hero because he could turn misfortune into benefit.

    D.   He was often laughed at and spat upon.

10. Describe Nasreddin Odjah's physical appearance.

    A.   He was a regal, well-coiffed gentleman with stately posture.

    B.   He was a well-groomed, finely dressed courtier.

    C.   He was a slightly overweight, white-bearded man who wore baggy clothes.

    D.   He was a dwarfed, hunch-backed, homunculus.

Questions About Vocabulary Terms in the Story

11. Nasreddin was educated in the teaching of the Koran. What is the Koran?

    A. The handbook about designer fashions

    B. A type of cookbook containing menus for wedding feasts

    C. The most widely used manual for physical exercises and nutrition at that time

    D. The sacred book composed of religious writings accepted by Muslims

12. Nasreddin changed the course of his homeward trek and went straight to the wedding supper. What is a trek?

    A. A vehicle specially designed for the rugged mountain terrain in Macedonia

    B. A trip that is sometimes slow and laborious, often involving difficulties or complex organization

    C. A class offered by an institution of higher learning

    D. A meal consisting of unappetizing food and drink

13. Baklava was served at the wedding feast. What is baklava?

    A. A dessert made of thin pastry, nuts, and honey

    B. A beefy main course that is baked for several days in advance

    C. A liver casserole that is spread between thick chunks of Bitola

    D. Heavily spiced, baked ribs of baby calves

14. Nasreddin Odjah poked some food into his cummerbund. What is a cummerbund?

    A. A large padded pocket designed to keep bread warm for long periods of time

    B. A harness designed to carry heavy instruments (generally worn over the shoulders)

    C. The band around a large, wide-brimmed hat

    D. A broad waistband worn in place of a vest

15. Near the end of the story a guest jumped to his feet and yelled, "*Effendi!*" What is the meaning of the word *Effendi*?

    A. It is an exclamatory expression often uttered after someone has been insulted.

    B. It is Macedonian slang for "enough."

    C. It is Macedonian for "sir."

    D. It is a command to stop whatever someone is doing at the moment.

II
Challenge Stories

Chapter 8

Leaving for America

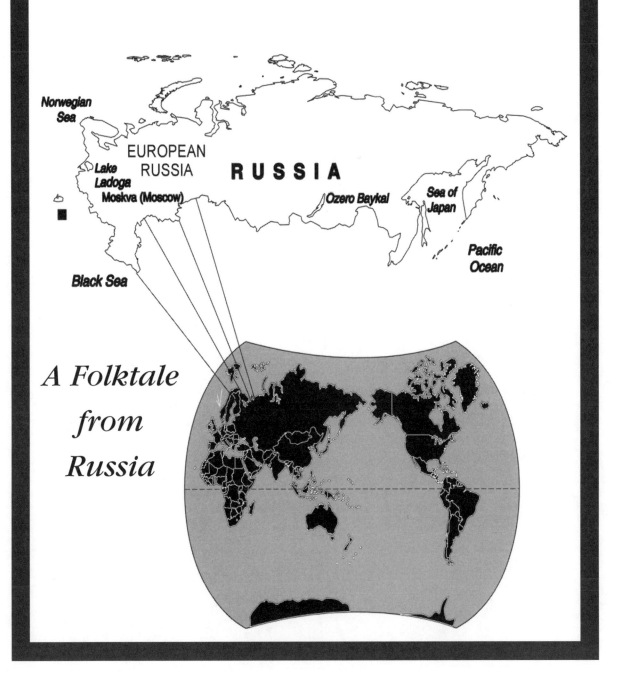

A Folktale

from

Russia

About the Contributor

This section was prepared primarily by

Roslyn Bresnick-Perry

Roslyn Bresnick-Perry was born in the little Russian Jewish town of Wysolie-Litewskie in 1922, and she came to America with her mother in 1929. Her extended family perished in the Holocaust in World War II. She grew up in New York City and struggled to overcome her family tragedy, together with culture shock, a language barrier, and dyslexia. After thirty-three years of working in the garment industry as a fashion designer, she graduated from college, completed an master's degree in cultural history, and ultimately found her niche as a professional storyteller. Her audiotape, *Holiday Memories of a Shtetl Childhood,* has been honored by the American Library Association as a Notable Recording for Children. The included story was first published as a children's book in 1992 by Children's Book Press.

Leaving for America (Russia)— Cultural Background

STORY GENRES

The stories included in Part I of this collection are all folktales that are an integral part of their associated cultures. In contrast, this selection is a *true* story, written from the viewpoint of a seven-year-old girl who actually experienced a journey to America to avoid the persecution of the Jews in Russia. This story style can be contrasted with the folktale genre, and the differences in narrative styles can be discussed with the listeners, if desired.

STORY BACKGROUND: BELARUS

The history of the country of Belarus hardly has a definite origin because the territories between the rivers Dnieper, Pripyat, Dvina, and Bug were inhabited from time immemorial. The first evidence of Slavic tribes living there date back to the first century A.D.

Belarus was and is a beautiful land of fertile fields and wonderfully untouched forests, dotted with many lakes, streams, and rivers. The land was constantly conquered and reconquered by the countries of Lithuania, Poland, and Russia in ferocious battles that devastated both the land and its people. Each country imposed its own culture, language, laws, religions, and demands upon the people of Byelorussia, who already spoke their own language and had their own way of life.

Although they were all a Slavic people and all had adopted Christianity from their previous pagan beliefs, these invasions were accompanied by wholesale massacres, bloodshed, destruction, and forced conversions to either the Orthodox Christian Church or to Catholicism.

JEWISH HISTORY IN BELARUS

Jewish merchants first visited Byelorussia in transit between Poland and Russia, and a community was established in 1506 in the city of Pinsk. The Christian citizenry consistently opposed the permanent settlements of Jews into the larger cities of those regions, although the Polish nobility welcomed them because of their experience in trade and industry. Smaller communities also grew up under the protection of Polish landowners who rented their towns, villages, taverns, or inns to Jewish contractors and made it possible for Jews fleeing from persecution to settle into those regions.

These small communities (which later developed into what became known as *shtetls*— towns and villages of various sizes) made constant attempts to break away from the jurisdiction of the older communities to manage their communal affairs independently.

People in these small communities established their own communal organizations for health, burial, and money-lending societies for their poor inhabitants. They established schools that taught Torah in Hebrew—a language that has been spoken since ancient times. (Torah is a collection of sacred books—the most important of which is the Hebrew Bible, known by many as the Old Testament.) Orphanages, marriage arrangements, Jewish holidays, and dietary laws were

developed. The people held fast to their history and cultural treasures—along with their own language (Yiddish), which evolved from a mixture of middle German and Hebrew and was written in the Hebrew alphabet. This language had traveled with them from the Rhineland, which had been their previous home. But most important to them was the Jewish religion, which they held onto with unswerving devotion, even when it meant death.

When the Russians ruled Byelorussia, their treatment of the Jewish population under their control was extremely harsh, with many injunctions and massacres called pogroms.

Although a small group of Jews acquired wealth through their participation in the establishment and trade of the various industries they helped to build, the vast majority of Jews living in the region of Byelorussia were relatively destitute.

The religious persecutions, the restrictions on their ability to participate in many industries and trades, the prohibition against their ownership of land, education, and civil rights collectively caused large numbers of Jews to emigrate to the Ukraine or southern Russia and to the United States beginning in the 1880s.

Who were the Jews and Why Were They Homeless? The Israelites (as they were once called) lived in a part of the Middle East that stood at the center of the ancient world. Their country was constantly overrun by the warring nations around them. They still managed to survive as a nation with their own religion (called Judaism) and with their holy temple in Jerusalem (built during the reign of King Solomon) until the Babylonians captured them, destroyed the Temple, and exiled them from their country.

Most of the Jews were taken to Babylonia and allowed to live there, but many Israelites left that part of the world and relocated to northern Africa, southern Europe, and many other places. Many became part of the culture of the various countries they inhabited, while others held onto their Judaism and continued adhering to the laws and dictates of their Holy Bible.

Several generations later, they were allowed to return to their own land of Israel where they rebuilt their temple and lived as a sovereign country until they were conquered by the

Romans (who destroyed their second temple and again exiled them from their land). A few Israelites managed to remain in their homeland, but the remainder settled in southern Europe around the Mediterranean Sea and farther up along the Rhine Valley (which was called the German Lands).

The Jews, as they were now called, kept their way of living their religion and were a society unto themselves. They refused to adopt Christianity—and thereby became the target for slander, persecution, death, and exile. Driven from country to country, they went wherever they were allowed.

 A note from Roslyn Bresnick-Perry: This is how my family ended up in Belarus. My father's great-great-great-grandfather was born in Belarus—although our family name was Kolner, the German name for a person who came from the city of Cologne (which was in the German lands).

 World War II broke out a few years after my mother and I left to join my father in America. The large families of both my parents remained in the town of Wysokie-Litewskie. During the war the Germans invaded that town, killing all its inhabitants—including all of our beloved family members. Our families were among the six million Jews killed in Europe in what is now called the Holocaust. After the war, the old new country of Israel was again established, and many Jewish people have gone back to their ancient homeland.

Leaving for America

A True Personal Story from Russia

By Roslyn Bresnick-Perry

Author's Note: I was born in a shtetl, a little Jewish town in Russia, many years ago. Times were hard for the Jews there, and when I was six months old my father left for America to make a better life for our family. It took him almost seven years of hard work to save enough money to bring my mother and me to America to join him. So I spent the first seven years of my life with my mother in our little town of Wysokie, without my father. Sometimes I would cry because my father was so far away, but he sent us letters and money and pictures of himself, and that made me feel better. This story is about my memories of those years and of my last days in Russia before leaving for America.

We were leaving for America. My mother and I were leaving our *shtetl*, our town of Wysokie, to join my father. Everyone had been talking about our going for so long that I thought the time would never come, but here it was, the very day.

We had said good-bye to friends, relatives, and neighbors two or three times each because we kept meeting them on the street or in the marketplace or at the synagogue. We had said good-bye so often that my mother finally stopped crying at each farewell.

I was sad to be leaving everyone, but something inside of me kept bubbling up with excitement, and I couldn't keep myself from smiling even though everyone else seemed so heavy-hearted.

Everyone made such a fuss over us. They invited us to have tea and cookies. They gave us advice and told my mother what to do and what not to do, who to get in touch with and who to be careful of.

"There are so many thieves in America," they said. They knew because their uncle or cousin or brother or sister who was there wrote to them about it. Everyone taught us the few words of English they knew. "You say 'yes' for *yo,* 'no' for *neyn,* and 'hokay' for everything else."

I said good-bye to my cousin Zisl when we left our house and went to stay with my grandmother and grandfather for the final few days before we were due to leave for America. My mother wanted to be with them until the very last moment because she had a terrible feeling we would never see them again.

I knew I would really miss Zisl. She was my best and worst friend. Sometimes we would love each other and sometimes we would fight. She used to get me into all kinds of trouble because she had so many ideas.

One time Zisl found a can of dark green paint and she wanted me to help her paint our old outhouse. I was wearing the new dress my father had sent me from America.

"Oh, I can't!" I cried. "My dress will get dirty and my mother will kill me!"

But Zisl had an answer right on the spot. "You can take off your dress and paint in your underwear."

"But everyone will see me in my underwear," I said, "and that's not nice."

"No, they won't either," said Zisl. "I'll watch out for you. Come on, stop being a crybaby. Let's go."

I got a good spanking for that adventure.

Zisl's family lived right next door to us. We used to tell each other all our secrets. I told her how I saw my Aunt Feygl kissing her boyfriend Srolke when she was supposed to be taking care of me. Everybody knew this was not allowed when you weren't married.

Right away Zisl got a gleam in her eye and said, "Let's tell Srolke that we're going to let the whole family know what they were doing unless he gives us a ride in his horse-drawn sleigh."

But Aunt Feygl and Srolke were getting married right after that, so they didn't care if everyone knew they were kissing. Srolke promised he would take us for a ride some day, but Zisl and I both knew he was always too busy to bother with us.

We never got our ride, but we had fun anyway by telling each other our dreams about flying to the moon in Srolke's sleigh. Zisl's dream was better than mine, and I didn't like that at all. But afterward I didn't care so much. I knew I would miss Zisl a lot.

On the day we were leaving for America, I woke up very early in the morning. A horse and wagon were already waiting for us at my grandparents' door. Grandfather and my Uncle Avrom-Leyb, my mother's youngest brother, were  carrying a large steamer trunk out of the house. Inside the trunk was everything that we were taking to America.

My mother had a hard time deciding what to take. She finally came to the conclusion that in America it would be impossible to get a feather bed like hers or the kind of linens she liked or such lovely embroidered underwear she was used to wearing, so she took all she had. She also took her copper pots and pans and her two silver candlesticks. Then when everything was packed, she put in her two wooden rolling pins, one on each side of the trunk.

Those rolling pins later created a sensation by falling out of the trunk during many immigration inspections we had to undergo upon arriving in America. The inspectors asked my mother if she had brought them along to use on her husband. Then they laughed and laughed at their own joke. We just stood there not knowing why they were laughing. When the joke was finally explained to my mother, she looked even more puzzled than before.

"Do women really hit their husbands with rolling pins in America?" she asked. "What a crazy land, America!"

On the morning we left for America, however, everything rested quietly in the trunk that Grandfather and Avrom-Leyb had loaded onto the wagon. I ran outside to watch every detail of what was going on. Everyone was crying. My mother, my Aunt Shuske, and my grandmother were standing by the wagon with their arms around each other, weeping without restraint. My Aunt Libe was in the house crying her eyes out. Aunt Feygl and Srolke cried silently, wiping their eyes and nose every few minutes. My grandfather comforted me, but he too was crying, his tears rolling out without a sound into his curly, honey-colored beard.

Seeing all the people of my world crying propelled me into hysterical sobbing. I cried the loudest, although only a few minutes before I had been filled with laughter and excitement. My grandmother, hearing my cries, tore herself out of my mother's arms, ran into the

house and was back in what seemed like a minute carrying a large slice of rye bread heaped high with chopped liver.

"*Na Mamele, es epis,*" she said. "Now darling, eat a little something so you'll feel better."

I ate my chopped liver crying with much less emotion. After all, how emotional can you be while eating chopped liver?

Everything was now ready for our departure. My mother had finally freed herself from all those loving arms and was sitting on the passenger seat of the wagon waiting for me. It was time to say good-bye to my grandfather.

I loved my grandfather. He was a tall, handsome, gentle man who always had a twinkle in his eyes and a smile on his lips whenever he saw me. Grandfather helped me learn my *Alef Beys,* my ABCs. He said that I must learn my letters so that I could read the Holy Books and the history of our people, and grow up knowing what is right and who I am.

Now it was time for us to leave. My grandfather reached over and started to lift me up to my mother in the wagon. But when I was in midair, he stopped and looked at me with great love and sadness.

"*Un du, mayn eynikl, du vest blaybn an emese yidishe tokhter?*" he whispered. "And you, my grandchild, will you remain a true Jewish daughter of your people?"

What a strange question, I thought, but I answered him cheerily. "*Avade, Zeyde.*" "Of course, Grandfather."

It has now been many years since the joyous day when my mother and I were united with my father in America. I am now a grandmother myself. But I have never forgotten my old home and all the wonderful people of my childhood. And I have never forgotten my grandfather's question. I share this story now to preserve the memory of my family and the little Jewish town in Russia where I grew up.

When people ask me if I still see Zisl, I sadly must tell them that Zisl died in the Holocaust when six million Jews were murdered during World War II. Then, all of a sudden, they become very quiet—because this thing that happened is not just "six million Jews," it's Zisl.

Stories are magical. They cross generations, they dissolve time and space, they overcome differences and barriers. When you hear someone's story, you can feel a connection, an empathy, a reaching out. That's why we must share our stories with one another. And that is why I share mine with you.

Coming to America (Russia)—
Follow-Up Information and Activities

DISCUSSION QUESTIONS

This true story of a young Jewish girl coming to America is more a description of an emotional journey than a fact-filled narrative of dates and places. Therefore, this follow-up section will involve several discussion questions instead of the multiple-choice items seeking an "accurate answer" (such as those following the earlier stories in this book). These question clusters can be prepared as activity cards and circulated among groups of two to five learners for discussion purposes. It is important to explain in advance that there are no right or wrong answers and that the opinions of others should be accepted and discussed without criticism. Explain also that this first-person story did not use the name of the little girl in its text, but that the storyteller's real name (Roslyn) will be used in these discussion questions. This helps avoid repetitions of "the little girl in the story," and it brings listeners closer to the realism of this historical event.

Roslyn was happy to move to America, but she was also sad. If you had to leave America and make another country your home, how would you feel? What would you miss most if you had to leave America? What would you look forward to in the new country? What types of general problems might a person encounter when moving to a new country?

Have you ever relocated to a faraway place, or have you known someone who has done so? If so, how did you or the person who relocated feel? How did the adults in the family react to the move? What important people were left behind? What important tangible objects were left behind?

Did you ever have to say good-bye to someone who has moved away? If so, how did you feel? How did that person feel? Did your feelings change as time passed? What would be different if you encountered that person again today?

Do you know a town, neighborhood, or district in your area where the people are very different from the majority of the population? If so, how are they treated? Do you think they are given fair treatment?

Why do you think Roslyn was so excited about leaving her country and yet did not allow herself to show it? Regarding leaving their country, what were the differences in the Roslyn's reactions and those of her mother? Why do you think Roslyn's mother thought she might never see her family again?

What did you learn from this story about the size of the *shtetl*—a place that made it possible for people to meet one another constantly in public areas? What did you learn about the community in Roslyn's hometown? Was it a stable place where people seldom wanted to leave?

Imagine you are in a place where people speak a language you do not understand? How would you handle a situation in which you were lost, had to buy something, or were put in a class in which your own language was not spoken?

How do you feel about people who speak with a foreign accent—as in saying "hokay" instead of "OK"? Do you laugh? Do you understand why there are so many language differences?

Roslyn described her cousin Zisl as her best and worst friend. What did she mean by that? Can a friend be both the best and the worst at the same time? How would you feel about having a friend who is also your cousin? Would it complicate the relationship?

Roslyn described a time when she was wearing her new American dress and Zisl wanted to paint the outhouse green. The two girls are dressed differently at that point in the story. A Yiddish expression (*Malbesh bi koved*) means "how you are dressed is the way you are viewed." Americans have a similar expression: "Clothes make the man." How important in your own culture is it to be dressed in a similar (or better) fashion than your friends or classmates? Have you ever felt inferior because you did not have expensive clothes?

Roslyn and Zisl's families used outhouses. They had no indoor toilet or plumbing, electricity, telephone, radio, television, or car. What kinds of activities would you and your friends enjoy under those circumstances? How do you think you could manage through the cold winter months without electric or gas heat?

Roslyn and Zisl lived next door to each other. The two girls told each other their secrets. What could that arrangement do to the privacy between the families? Can you foresee any problems with such behavior?

In the *shtetl*, marriages were usually arranged between families. How would you feel if your family decided who your marriage partner would be?

Zisl and Roslyn became mischievous when they saw their Aunt Faygl kissing her boyfriend. What do you think could have happened if they had told other family members what they saw? Could they have done any damage to these young lovers? Would you be tempted to "squeal" if you knew someone in your family had broken such a rule?

Winter in the shtetl was both magnificently beautiful and horribly disastrous because the only means of transportation was the horse and wagon. Only the wealthy had sleighs. The attempted blackmail of Roslyn's aunt (to go for a ride in a horse-drawn sleigh or squeal about her kissing her boyfriend) was quite an ambitious demand. What problems would you have if you had no transportation other than walking or a rare sleigh ride?

On the day Roslyn and her mother were ready to leave for America, they had all of their possessions in a trunk. If you had to leave your hometown and had only one trunk in which to place your possessions, which items would you include?

The inspectors joked about the falling rolling pins. Why did they think this was funny? Why didn't Roslyn's mother see the humor in their joke? What does this say about the American culture?

People who had relatives living in America had advised Roslyn and her mother to be careful because "There are so many thieves in America." Do you think their conclusion was an accurate one? How do you think people from other countries view America?

How do people in other countries develop their ideas about Americans? How can people from different countries get to know each other? What might be the best way today for people to communicate between countries?

When Roslyn and her mother were ready to leave for America, Roslyn suddenly began crying louder than everyone else. Her grandmother gave her a slice of rye bread heaped with chopped liver. Have you ever eaten chopped liver? Do any of your relatives offer you food when you are feeling low? Do you think food can calm your emotions or affect your emotional well-being? What is your favorite food to eat when you feel stressed out?

Roslyn hated to leave her grandfather because he had been a surrogate father, teacher, and transmitter of her heritage. Has there been such an influential person in your life? If so, describe that person.

Roslyn's grandfather asked her if she would remain a true Jewish daughter of her people. What did he mean by that question? Why do you think he asked her this? Why do you think Roslyn never forgot the question? What did it mean to her?

Roslyn came to America knowing only three words: no, yes, and OK. What do you think it would be like to move to a new country knowing only three words? What steps would you take to learn the new language? Would that be easy or difficult for you? Have you ever met anyone who could not speak English? If so, how did you communicate with them?

Large numbers of people immigrated to American at the beginning of the twentieth century. Why did they come to America at that time? From which countries did they come? What were some of the problems they experienced? How did Americans treat them?

At the end of the twentieth century, large numbers of people began immigrating to America again. Why? From which countries did they come? What are some of the problems they are experiencing? How are Americans treating them now?

Chapter 9

The Coal Basket

A Folktale

from

Scotland

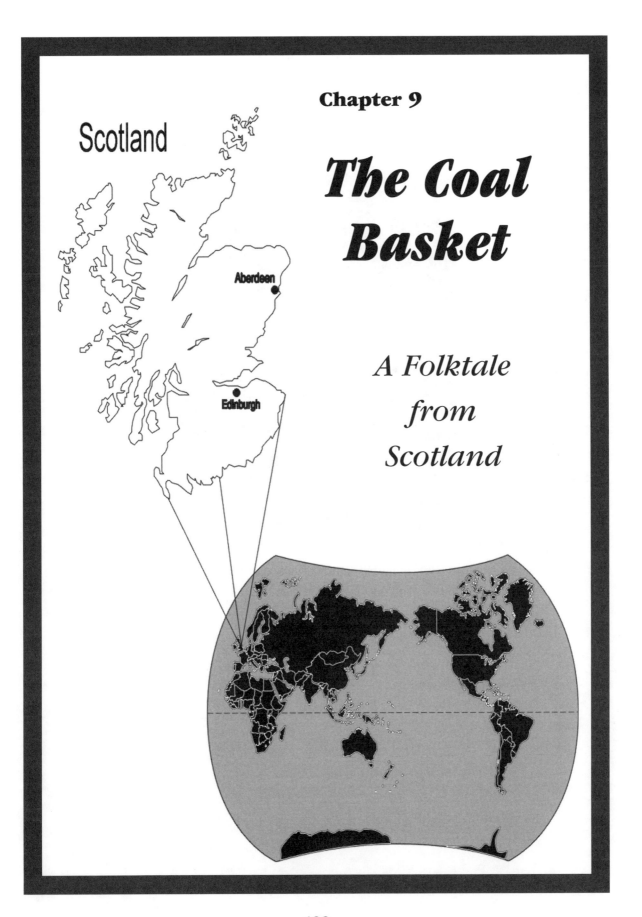

Scotland

Aberdeen

Edinburgh

About the Contributor

This section was prepared primarily by

Wendy Welch

Wendy Welch lives with her husband, traditional Scottish singer Jack Beck, in a farming village near the North Sea in Scotland, an ideal setting for peaceful contemplation and relaxed writing—none of which she can do because she has to drive up and down the country like a mad fiend to keep up with her storytelling bookings. She runs the nonprofit, charity organization, *Storytelling Unplugged*, which uses storytelling for problem-solving purposes in the areas of education, the environment, therapy, and developmental arts. Wendy has a Ph.D. in folklore and has lived and performed in many different parts of the world. Her Web site is www.scottishsongandstory.co.uk.

The Coal Basket (Scotland)— Cultural Background

BACKGROUND FACTS FOR SCOTLAND

Scotland is a country that is part of a union of nations called the United Kingdom. People often assume that England, Great Britain, and the United Kingdom are synonymous (the same thing), and certainly the differences can be confusing for people who don't live in the UK. This is how it is: Wales, England, and Scotland together make up Great Britain; these three countries and Northern Ireland are the United Kingdom.

Scottish people speak English, and many also speak Gaelic, Scots, or both. Gaelic is heard in the North, while people in Central Scotland use Scots. Margaret and her family speak Scots in the story *The Coal Basket*.

Coal mining used to be an important occupation in Scotland; at the beginning of the 1980s there were more than thirty mines across the country. The strike in this story was only one of several "industrial actions," as they are called in Britain. It is probably one of the two most famous strikes of all time. The second famous strike took place in 1984, and it had severe consequences. When the strike was over, most mines remained closed, so miners had to find other work. The last deep coal mine in Scotland was called Longannet, and it closed following an accident in 2002. No one was killed, but the mine filled with water and became unusable. Today there are no working mines in Scotland.

Scotland still relies heavily on farming and fishing for its own food and for sale to other countries. It is also a popular place for people from around the world to take their vacations (holiday-makers, they are called in the UK). Scotland is known for having lively music and dancing, and many people who have Scottish ancestors in their families like to research their names.

In North America, many families are Scottish because of the Highland Clearances. This happened in the early 1800s. Thousands of farmers (who would be called sharecroppers in the United States) were told to move to the coast and change their occupation to fishing because the people who owned the land wanted to use it to raise sheep. Most of these poor farmers couldn't figure out how to make a living by fishing, so they decided to move away and start over. They went to Canada, Australia, and the United States.

Also, Scotsmen were renowned for being excellent fighters, and countries that couldn't raise their own armies often hired them. Many of the people who fought in the American Revolution were Scottish. Sometimes these soldiers got married and stayed in the New World. These are two reasons why Scottish music and stories are so popular around the world; there is a Scot in almost every country!

Tartan, the plaid cloth that is often associated with Scotland, is also popular all over the world. The different patterns of tartan are believed to represent family names. If your last name is Cameron, "your" tartan is yellow and black; Ferguson tartan is yellow and green. But these tartans are not ancient ways of telling families apart, as is sometimes represented on television or by businesspeople who want to sell them. Queen Victoria, who was English but loved Scotland and spent a lot of time there, invented them in the mid-1800s. She was trying to do something useful, but "tartan mania" embarrasses many people in Scotland.

Scotland in movies and films is often shown only in the past. Modern movies about Scottish life are not often screened outside Scotland, while movies such as *Braveheart* and *Rob Roy* have been popular in many countries. This sometimes gives the idea that Scotland has a romantic interest in the past and is not an active country in politics—an image many people in Scotland want to change!

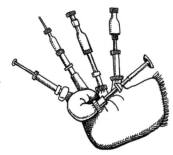

Bagpipe music, fiddles, and accordions are probably the most common instruments people think of as Scottish, and during the summer months there are many festivals showcasing this music. Scottish foods such as haggis and neeps are served during these festivals. Neeps are turnips, usually served mashed like potatoes. Haggis is made of different kinds of grains, like barley and wheat, wrapped inside the intestine of a sheep. Many people don't like haggis.

PRONUNCIATION GUIDE

Those who choose to read the following story may wonder about how to pronounce some of the words. Much of Scots is pronounced as it is spelled; it is largely a spoken rather than written language. Here are a few exceptions:

Sounds ending in "oo" in English (do, to) end in a long *a* in Scots: tae = tay; dae = day.

"Not" becomes "nae"—again with a long *a* sound: wasn't = wisnae (wiz-nay); don't = disnae (dih-nay); can't = cannae (can-nay).

Any long vowel sounds in verbs usually become short: take = tak (tack); make = mak (mac); break = brak (brack)

"Ou" or "ow" sounds become "ooh" sounds: out = oot; houses = hooses. "How are you?" becomes "Hoo ye daein?"

Sounds like "augh" become "awkt": daughter = dochter (dawkter); brought = brokt (brawkt).

"Polis" has the accent on the first syllable.

The "igh" sounds (as in "night") becomes "ik" pronounced like "nickel": night = nicht (nicked). This is exactly like the German sound; this phoneme is not found in the English language.

Most "ing" endings drop to "in'."

"Gin" in Scots is pronounced with a hard *g* (as in "gift") not like the drink!

For the remainder of the words, pronounce them according to your own phonics generalizations.

The Coal Basket

An Oral History Tale from Scotland

Retold by Wendy Welch

This story weaves together several true events from the lives of people who survived the Great Strike of 1926. Margaret Meikleham is a fictional character; the things that happened to her in the story actually happened to many people during the strike. Mrs. McKinness (that was not her real name) did lose two sons in the way described, and the money sent to buy food for hungry families is also true. The story was originally told to Wendy by Davy Lockhart, whose uncles were the brothers killed in the mine.

Margaret Jean Meikleham was thirteen years old and hungrier than she had ever been in her life. Eight months earlier, Margaret had worked at the pithead, picking stones out of the coal as it passed by on the conveyor belt. She'd had this job since she finished school. It wasn't work she loved; it wasn't work she hated; it was just work to be done. Sometimes she daydreamed, but mostly she watched the coal. Daydreaming meant missing stones, and Margaret's family needed the money she brought home.

Now the pit was silent, the conveyor belt still. Her father, her uncle, all her friends' fathers were done going to meetings and coming home with angry faces. Everyone in the town said it was a time for action. This confused Margaret, for the General Strike[1] was inaction; the coal miners stopped work. Up and down the row houses people sat on their front steps or stood outside the High Street shops, where only women pushing prams went on a weekday. It made Margaret feel funny to see the men standing there.

Back then the shop windows were full of leaflets, screeching, "Not a penny off the wage, not a minute on the day!" Margaret remembered asking her father what it meant. "The mine owners are tryin' tae cut oor wages, wantin' mair wark fer less pay, an' we're sayin' no!"[2]

Margaret was surprised; she only brought home twelve shillings[3] a week. "But we cannae live on less!" she said. Her father smiled, but it wasn't a real smile. "I ken. Ye ken. It's the government that has tae ken. We'll mak them lissen, lass, ye an' me an' the ithers."[4]

Margaret felt proud to be a part of the plan to make the government listen. And, although she never said so, she liked having the time off with her friend Nancy.

---

1. The 1926 strike in Great Britain involved several "labor" professions, including bus drivers, steel workers, and miners. It began on May 4. The other workers went back to their jobs on May 12, but the miners continued to strike through November.

2. "The mine owners are trying to reduce our wages, wanting more work for less pay, and we're saying no!"

3. A shilling is about a dollar, equivalent to the minimum wage in Scotland today.

4. Cannae = can't. "I know. You know. It's the government that has to know. We'll make them listen, honey, you and me and the other miners."

Nancy lived across town and worked for another mine. They'd been best friends at school, but since then met only at church or miners' picnics. Now they sat and talked about the strike—and about  Adam Lockhart, so strong he could lift two baskets of coal at once. He smiled at Nancy whenever they met. Margaret wished he would smile at her like that.

But as the General Strike wore on, nobody smiled. The steel workers and bus drivers went back to their jobs. The voices of the people in the High Street[5] were lower now, and angry, snarling that the coal miners had been betrayed. One of the shops closed. Adam Lockhart walked with a face like stone, jaw clenched and eyes hooded. So did the rest of the miners.

Margaret remembered, as her stomach rumbled, the day her mother told her to leave the dinner dishes, she would clear them herself. But Margaret, returning to the kitchen to ask a question, saw her mum put the bits left from the plates into a pot. Margaret opened her mouth, then shut it. She sneaked away before her mother saw her.

 Sitting on the front step, listening to her belly growl, Margaret knew she wouldn't scorn "leftover soup" now if they had it. And although she tried to

shut it out, her memory played out the rest of that night.

Startled by what she had seen in the kitchen, Margaret went to Nancy's house. It was a late summer evening; a chill was in the air. In the strong summer sunlight,[6] Margaret could see no movement at Nancy's terraced cottage.

The house windows had been covered with mesh, boards nailed across the doors. Each bore the notice: "NO TRESPASSING by order of FIFE COAL COMPANY." A few of the windows were broken.

Margaret's heart beat painfully against her chest. It was like looking at a graveyard. She ran back to her house, bursting in the door. "Daddy! Daddy!"

Her mother sprang up. "He's no' here, Margaret. Whit's wrang?"[7]

"Nancy's awa'! A' the hooses are shut, an' there's a notice—" Her mother came forward and with a quick movement wrapped Margaret in her arms. "Ach, lassie, I didnae ken ye'd gang there the nicht, or I'da telt ye." She pulled back, looked into her

---

5. The High Street is the equivalent of "downtown" or the main shopping district of each town. The street with the shops is always called High Street, and it is often a pedestrian-only district.

6. Scotland is so close to the North Pole that it remains daylight during the summer until as late as 11 P.M., and in winter it is dark by 3 P.M. at some times.

7. "He's not here, Margaret. He's off to a meeting. What's wrong?"

daughter's face. "Sit doon, bairnie." They sat at the table. Her mother fidgeted with her hands, then without looking at her said, "Ye're no' a bairn ony mair, Margaret. Ye're auld eneuch' tae ken whit's happenin'. The ither mine turned the warkers oot o' their tied hooses. Gin they're no' warkin' for the mines, they cannae hae the hooses, the mine owners say."[8]

Margaret said in desperation, "But Nancy's mum was expectin'!"

Mrs. Meikleham pushed herself back from the table. "An' still is. They're no' deid, dochter, they're only awa' frae hame. They've gaen tae live elsewhere until they kin live here again. Haud yer wheesht."[9] Margaret scrubbed the tears from her eyes with her sleeve, embarrassed that her mother had seen them.

When her father came home, Margaret was waiting up. She reached for the coin purse to put money in the gas meter for lights.[10] The purse was empty.

"We're needin' tae be sparin'," he said in a flat tone, and Margaret stopped. "Daddy, whaur are the miners frae across the toun? Nancy an' a'? They're turned oot o' their hooses."[11]

"Dinnae worry. They're livin' in the caves the ither side o' the valley. They're safer than we are. Gang tae bed, bairnie." Margaret got up, but her father's voice rose suddenly in the dark room. "Maggie! Lissen noo'. This is important. Fer the next wee while, stay close tae the hoose. Dinnae gae aff tae the caves an' the like. Yer mum needs ye, an'—an' I said bide near the hoose. Dinnae speir; jist dae as ye're telt."[12]

The next day, warning or not, Margaret tried to find the caves. But as she neared Nancy's old house, she heard shouting and saw an angry mob standing outside the terraced row. To her surprise, she saw her own gentle father among them, his face purple with rage, his fists shaking in the air with the rest. She hung back so he wouldn't see her, but all eyes were on a group of men carrying boxes into the cottages and the police officers standing by, watching impassively.

At the edge of the crowd, she saw Adam Lockhart. Normally she would have been too shy to speak to him, but she was desperate. "Adam! Whit's this?"

---

8. "Nancy's gone! All the houses are closed up, and there's a notice—" . . . "Oh, sweetie, I didn't know you'd go there tonight, or I'd have told you." . . . "Sit down, child." . . . "You're not a child any more, Margaret. You're old enough to know what's happening. The other mine evicted the workers, because they lived in tied houses [houses that belonged to the mine and were rented to the workers as part of their wages]. If they're not working for the mines, they can't live in the houses, the mine owners say."

9. "She still is. They're not dead, daughter, they're only evicted. They've gone to live somewhere else until they can come back. Stop crying."

10. Houses were heated by coal fireplaces, but lights were gas. Most houses had coin-operated meters; if you wanted lights in the evening, you paid as you used the gas.

11. "We need to conserve fuel," . . . "Daddy, where are the miners from across town? Nancy and all? They've been evicted."

12. "Don't worry. They're living in the caves on the other side of the valley. They're safer than we are. Go to bed, child." . . . "Maggie! Listen carefully. This is important. Stay close to the house for the next few days. Don't go off to the caves and other places. Your mom needs you, and—and I said to stay near the house. Don't ask questions; just do as you're told."

"Blacklegs," he said, biting off the word as though it tasted bad. "Stinkin' blackleg miners."

Margaret sneaked back home, afraid to pass her father and the mob, and more confused than ever. All miners had black legs—and arms, and faces—because of coal dust. Some even had a disease called Black Lung when the dust got inside them; her grandfather had died from that. Was black legs another disease? Why would people yell at a group of poor sick miners?

When she got home it was midday, but the family had stopped eating dinner more than a month ago. Breakfast and tea,[13] her mother said, was enough for anyone. "Mum," she asked, "whit's a blackleg?"

Her mum's face grew hard. "Were ye awa' frae the hoose the day?" Margaret looked away. Her mother sighed. "A blackleg is someone brocht frae anither place tae wark. They men in the row hooses where Nancy lived cam frae Ireland tae wark the coal. Strike-breakers. But gin they dae that. . ." Her voice faltered. ". . . there'll be fichtin'. I dinnae want ye far frae hame these days, Margaret."[14]

Not long after this, police whistles shrilled in the night and Margaret sat up in bed. From the street she heard running footsteps. A door slammed. Voices spoke in agitated whispers. But when Margaret got up to investigate, her mother's voice rang harsh and rough across the darkened front room. "Get back tae yer bed! Noo!"[15] In all her life, Margaret had never heard her soft-spoken mother sound like that. She fled.

The next morning there was no sign of Daddy. Margaret's mother moved around the house like a ghost—dusting, sitting with her hands in her lap, dusting the same places again. Donald and Mary tried to light a fire in the cold grate. Her mother seemed not to hear. Margaret knew that there was little fuel left. She wrapped her younger brother and sister in a blanket each, sat down and began to tell them a story.

A knock sounded on the door, and Mrs. Meikleham jumped straight into the air. Two policemen entered without waiting to be admitted. "Does Donald Meikleham live here?"

"Aye," said her mother, "but he's awa'. He's aff tae find work in Aiberdeen. His brother lives there."[16] Margaret tried to keep her face still. She'd never heard Mum lie before.

The policemen looked at her mother in a way Margaret didn't like, then one of

---

13. The evening meal in Scotland is called tea; the midday meal is dinner.

14. "Were you far from the house today?" . . . "A blackleg is someone brought in from another place to work. Those men in the row houses [a row of four to six houses that share walls—like one long building, but each one being a private house] where Nancy lived came from Ireland to work the coal. Strike-breakers. But if they succeed, there will be riots. I don't want you far from home these days, Margaret."

15. "Get back in bed this instant!"

16. "Yes but he's not here. He's gone to find work in Aberdeen [a large town in the northeast of Scotland that does not have coal mining]. His brother lives there."

them gave a kindly smile. "There's nae need tae be feart. We're only speirin' after information. He's in nae trouble."[17]

Mrs. Meikleham drew herself up. "My husband disnae mak trouble."[18]

The men left. Margaret and the little ones rushed to her mother, clamoring questions. She raised her hands. "Wheesht! Wheesht, bairnies! Let yer puir mither think!"[19]

"Where is Daddy?" Mary cried.

"He's awa' tae Aiberdeen," her mother answered, pulling the little girl onto her lap. "He's awa' tae find wark. An' he'll send a bawbee fer ye tae gae tae the shop an' buy sweeties. Noo wheest yer speirin'." And she rocked her youngest daughter back and forth.[20]

Margaret knew better than to ask her mother any more in front of the little ones, so she went to the High Street and asked old Tam at the newsagent's shop what was going on. Tam eyed her, then said, "There was trouble here the nicht. A group o' them blacklegs an' a group o' oor miners focht. A blackleg was killed, an' men hurt on a' sides. The polis cam oot. Some o' oor men fled."[21]

Margaret felt sick to her stomach. Her father would have nothing to do with fight-

ing, with killing, she was sure. But where was he? "Ta,"[22] she said, and left the shop.

Weeks passed. The days were getting shorter and colder, but there was no coal for heat. Chairs began disappearing. Not a scrap of wood was left anywhere on the streets. Mrs. Meikleham sometimes answered the door to find a miner standing there with a few bits of coal. "Tae warm the bairnies until yer man comes hame,"[23] they'd say, shuffling their feet and avoiding her eyes.

The hens in the back garden were good layers, and there were always eggs. But one day there were four hens instead of five, then three. And the day came when breakfast wasn't on the table. Mrs. Meikleham said in a cheerful voice, "Here's a mug o' tea each, and we'll hae a braw denner. Nae need for tea gin ye hae a braw denner!"[24]

Donald and Mary cried sometimes, soft snuffling whimpers like puppies. They were hungry. At lunch one day Margaret saw her mother take the bread from her own plate, divide it in half, and call out, "Wha's that in the front garden?" When the children looked, she put the bread on their plates. "Och! It mustae been the breid fairy! Look whit she's left!"[25]

Margaret took the slice from her own plate. "She's left me a hale one, but Ah'm

---

17. "There's no need to be frightened. We're only asking a few questions. He's not in trouble."

18. "My husband doesn't make trouble."

19. "Hush! Hush, children! Let your poor mother think!"

20. "He's gone to Aberdeen," . . . "He's gone to look for a job. And he'll send you a penny so you can go to the store to buy candy. Now stop asking me all these questions."

21. "There was trouble here last night. A group of blackleg miners and a group of our miners had a fight. A blackleg was killed, and men hurt on both sides. The police came. Some of our men fled."

22. "Thanks"

23. "To keep the children warm until your husband comes home"

24. "Here's a mug of tea each, and we'll have a nice big midday meal. No need for an evening meal if you have a good lunch!"

25. "Who's that in our front yard?" . . . "Oh! It must have been the bread fairy! Look what she's left!"

no' hungry. Here." She divided it in half for Donald and Mary. After the meal, her mother pulled her aside. "Ye're a guid lass, Margaret, but ye'r growin'," she said, giving her a hug. Margaret could feel her trembling. "Eat yer ain breid. Ah'm auld an' dinnae need tae get fat."[26]

And at last the day Margaret had dreaded came. Two boiled eggs sat on the dinner table. Margaret looked at her mother. Her mother met her eye. "Ah'm aff tae Nancy's hoose, then," Margaret said out loud. "Ah'll hae my tea there." Her mother nodded. "Ah've already eaten. Noo ye twa, tuck in. Here's an egg each."[27]

Now Margaret Jean Meikleham, aged thirteen, sat on her front porch and listened to her stomach rumble. Inside the house, she could hear Mary crying. Her mother was lying down. She spent a lot of time lying down these days.

From up the street came a voice. "Haw, Maggie!" Mrs. McKinness, the widow, hailed her. Mrs. McKinness was famous for her sons. Ewan had been twenty-six when his younger brother Michael was sixteen. Working side by side in the mines one day, they heard a soft creak of timber. Ewan grabbed Michael and threw him just as a great wall of rock fell where Michael had been a moment before. Ewan was crushed.

The older miners who retold the tale nodded. "Ye kin live an' die by the creak o' the timbers. Ewan was a guid miner."[28]

But the saddest part of the story, Margaret thought, came later. Michael enlisted as a soldier in the Great War[29] and was dead six months after Ewan. Albert McKinness, the youngest, had emigrated, fleeing in the middle of the night so the mine manager couldn't stop him. Now, every month, Mrs. McKinness received a stiff white envelope with an international money order from Canada.

Margaret once said to her mother that she thought Ewan's act had been for nothing. Her mother considered, wiping her hands on the dishtowel in front of the sink. "Naethin' a body daes for guid is ivver wasted. Ewan lookit efter his brother, an' that was guid; maybe it maks ithers want tae be guid."[30]

Margaret didn't think so, but she held her tongue.

Now Mrs. McKinness was calling, "Maggie! Can ye come ower a minute?" Neighbours with nothing to do looked on

26. "She's left me a whole one, but I'm not hungry. Here." . . . "You're a good girl, Margaret, but you're growing," . . . "Eat your own bread. I'm old and don't need to get fat."

27. "I'm going to Nancy's for lunch," Margaret said out loud. "I'll have supper there too." . . . "I've already eaten. Now you two, tuck in. Here's an egg each."

28. Haw = hello. "You can live or die by the creaking of the timbers. Ewan was a good miner." Underground mines were held up with large timber frames. Sometimes the wood creaked as rock or timbers shifted and settled, and experienced miners could tell by the sounds if this was dangerous or not. Ewan, hearing the wood creak in a particular way, knew that bit of the mine was going to collapse and threw his brother to safety. Small collapses such as this one were common, and did not always result in deaths. Larger collapses were not unknown, but were much more serious.

29. World War I

30. "Nothing a person does for good is ever wasted. Ewan looked after his brother, and that was good; maybe it makes people who hear about it want to be good."

in idle interest as Mrs. McKinness held out a basket covered with a cloth. "It's auld breid, ower hard tae eat. Fer the hens."[31] Margaret thanked her and carried the heavy basket home. If there was that much stale bread, perhaps some of it was still edible. At least it would give the wee ones something to chew.

She went into the house, shut the door, set the basket on the table, and lifted the cover. Inside were a loaf of bread, several slices of ham, a jar of preserves, two round cheeses, and some turnips. A packet of tea nestled beside the bread; four carrots peeked out from under the cheeses.

"Mum! MUM!" Margaret shrieked. Her mother appeared, startled, and Margaret dragged her by the hand to where Donald and Mary stood, eyeing the basket with awe. Her mother stared at the food, then at her children. "Where did ye get this?"

"Mrs. McKinness. She said it was auld breid fer the chickens."

"We cannae . . ." she looked at the two youngest children, their eyes round and wide as they stared at the basket, at their mother, at the basket. Mrs. Meikleham swallowed, then walked from the room. Margaret reached into the basket and pulled out the bread. She sliced the loaf and gave each child a thick piece topped with ham.

Her mother returned. In her hands was a doily embroidered with butterflies. "Put this in the basket when ye tak it back. Dinnae let the neebors see it,"[32] she said.

That night they ate turnip soup. Three days later a thick letter arrived with an Aberdeen postmark. When her mother read it, her face dimpled. "Yer faither's sent rail tickets. He's fund a job. We'll gang the morn."[33]

And they went, leaving Nancy and the others in the caves and the blackleg miners to their work. The strike folded two months later; the miners crept back to their jobs with their pay cut. "A' fer naethin'," her father said, crumpling the newspaper in his fist. "Seeven months o' starvin' an' freezin' an' everyone aye angry an' a' fer what?"[34]

Without thinking, Margaret tugged at her father's sleeve. "It wisnae a' bad, Daddy. There wis Mrs. McKinness's basket," she said.

Her father's face as he looked at her was so frightening that Margaret regretted her words. Then he pulled her against him, and she could feel the rough stubble of his cheek against her forehead. "Aye, bairnie, an' sae lang as ye live, dinnae forget Mrs. McKinness's basket. An' when ye grow up, gin ye hae ocht tae spare, mind ye gie it tae someone."[35]

---

31. Ower = over. "It's stale bread, too hard to eat. Feed it to your hens."

32. Cannae = can't; tak = take; dinnae = don't

33. "Your father's sent tickets for the train to Aberdeen. He's found a job. We'll leave tomorrow." Mr. Meikleham probably became a dockworker unloading fish from the boats. Most of Scotland is connected by railways, which were and still are a common way of moving about.

34. "Seven months of starving and freezing and everybody mad all the time, for nothing?" wasnae = wasn't; wis = was

35. "Yes dear, and as long as you live, don't forget Mrs. McKinness's basket. And when you grow up, if you have anything to spare, see that you give it to someone."

The Coal Basket (Scotland)—
Follow-Up Information and Activities

MATCH THESE NAMES WITH THEIR DESCRIPTIONS

Robert Burns   National poet of Scotland, wrote many famous songs in Scots

Ewan McGregor   Movie actor from Scotland

William Wallace   Leader of rebellion against English king who set the ground on fire in a brilliant military move

Loch Ness Monster   Famous tourist attraction (that may or may not exist)

Andrew Carnegie   Philanthropist and steel factory owner who endowed libraries around the world

Robert the Bruce   Scottish king inspired by a spider to keep trying to repel the English from Scotland

Mary Queen of Scots   Scottish monarch beheaded by a cousin on a trumped-up charge

Each one of the above has an interesting life story. Investigate their lives on the Internet or in your library and see what you can learn about them.

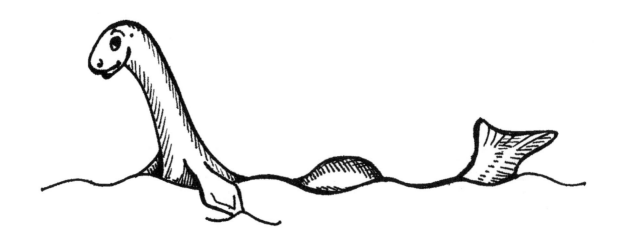

The Coal Basket (Scotland)—
Follow-Up Information and Activities

SINGING FUN

Children in Scotland love this song. It is sung to the tune of "She'll Be Coming 'Round the Mountain." (*Cannae* is pronounced "can-nay"; *aff* as in "after"; *yer* as in "yurt.") Have fun singing this with your friends. Make up your own verses about what (or who) can and cannae be shoved aff a bus!

Oh ye cannae shove yer granny aff a bus
Oh ye cannae shove yer granny aff a bus
Oh ye cannae shove yer granny, for she's yer mammie's mammie
Oh ye cannae shove yer granny aff a bus

Oh ye cannae shove yer uncle aff a bus
Oh ye cannae shove yer uncle aff a bus
Oh ye cannae shove yer uncle, he's got a big carbunkle (a corn on the foot)
Oh ye cannae shove yer uncle off a bus

Ye can shove yer ither granny aff a bus
Ye can shove yer ither granny aff a bus
Ye can shove yer ither granny, for she's yer daddie's mammie
Ye can shove yer ither granny aff a bus.

The Coal Basket (Scotland)—
Follow-Up Information and Activities

SOME POINTS TO PONDER

What is the difference between Great Britain and the United Kingdom?_____

_____

_____

Why do Scottish people have a love-hate relationship with tartan? _____

_____

_____

What were the Highland Clearances? _____

_____

_____

What instruments are the most popular in Scotland? _____

_____

_____

What are the main languages spoken in Scotland? _____

_____

_____

Why is coal mining no longer an important industry in Scotland?

_____

_____

What is haggis? _____

_____

_____

Give two reasons why there are Scottish people all over the world. _____

_____

_____

What is Black Lung Disease? _____

_____

_____

How is a Scottish summer day different from an American summer day?_____

_____

_____

What is the Scots word for "if"? _____

_____

_____

Why did Mrs. Meikleham put a lace doily in the basket of "auld bried"? _____

_____

_____

Why did Mrs. McKinness pretend the basket had "auld bried" in it? _____

_____

_____

How long was the General Strike for the coal miners? _____

_____

_____

The Coal Basket (Scotland)—
Follow-Up Information and Activities

SCOTLAND AND YOU: THE BIGGER PICTURE

Politics. Scotland is one country inside a union of four countries. That means that Scotland makes some decisions about itself, and the bigger union government makes the rest. What are some decisions made by your state government, and what are some made by the federal government? Research this and make a list in two columns on a display poster.

Stereotypes. Scotland finds tourism very important financially. However, the tourist industry relies on some stereotypes of the country, like tartan, that are not really how Scottish people feel about themselves. What stereotypes are associated with your region or state that do not accurately reflect how you think about yourselves?

Tourism. (1) Does your area receive many tourists? When do they come (summer, fall, etc.)? Are there particular events that attract these tourists? Do the newspapers and television stations in your area cover these events? If so, what do they say about them? From how far away do people come to visit? Write a news report about a tourist event in your area. You can do this either after going to the festival or by looking at information from your newspaper or on the Internet. You might also want to talk to your local chamber of commerce.

(2) If your area does not have much tourism, why do you think it doesn't? What is "popular" about your area that you could show to people from someplace else? Design a festival around this. Decide what foods you would sell, what kinds of arts and crafts you would show, and whether you would have music, dancing, storytelling, or other activities.

(3) Is there a "legend" about your area? Do you have a sea serpent, a mysterious something in the woods, flying saucer sightings? Are these popular with tourists, or only local residents? Debate the existence of your local mystery, or of the Loch Ness Monster.

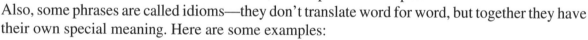

Language. (1) Scots sounds a lot like English, but some words are very different. For instance "greetin' " means crying, "speir" means to ask, and "steer" means a fuss or bother, a "tempest" is a teapot. Also, some phrases are called idioms—they don't translate word for word, but together they have their own special meaning. Here are some examples:

"Ah'm fair skunnert wi' it!" (I'm fed up!)

"Dinnae fash yersel'." (Don't get upset.)

"Naebody did it tae me, it wis my ainsel'!" (Nobody did it to me, it was my own fault!)

What idioms (or phrases that don't mean what they literally say word for word) do you use in your own speech? See if your parents or grandparents and people their age use different ones, and if they know the ones that you use.

(2) One of the problems with keeping Scots alive as a language is that different regions of Scotland speak it so differently; they call the same language by different names! In the Northeast, it is Doric; in the South, Lallans. Scots is very fragmented, very divided up into different dialects from different areas. Think about the way people where you live speak. Do you use any words that are not common in other places? Do you have a particular way of speaking that could be called an accent? Write down words and phrases that are considered local.

Employment or Industry. (1) Think about the people you know in your area. Where do most of them work? Are there big places that employ lots of people in your area? Do people work in offices? In factories? What kinds of jobs do your classmates' parents have? Prepare an informal survey and interview several of your classmates about the above items. Present your findings in an interesting manner (charts, graphs, etc.).

(2) What are the big industries of your region or state? How long have they been important? How has this changed in the last one hundred years? Do you think these industries will still be important one hundred years from now? Why or why not?

(3) Are there mines in your area? If so, what products are being mined? What are the working conditions like for the employees? If there are no mines in your area, investigate the history of coal mining in the United States. What were the working conditions? How were people paid? Did men and women both work? If so, how were their jobs different?

(4) Have there been any strikes in your area? There have been many famous strikes in America, including newspapers, mines, and teamsters. Research a strike relevant to your state, your school, or your family. Prepare a dramatic role-playing activity with both strikers and management as the actors.

Media. How is your region represented in films and books? Are there any movies about your area? Have any movies been set in your area with a different theme? Investigate books, films, or other art forms that present your region to the reading and viewing public. How accurate do you think these portrayals are? Are there descriptions of places you know? If so, are they correct? If you are from a place that does not have any books or films involving it, select another area with which you have connections. Keep in mind that it is important to choose a place you know or have access to, because you cannot compare the media descriptions with reality unless you know the reality!

A Final "Good Deed." Think about people you know in your area who might be close to the hunger level the Meiklehams faced in this story. Pretend you will be preparing a "basket" to give to them. What items would you collect for this basket? How would you present it to them in a manner that prevented their being embarrassed by accepting it? How will you feel as a result?

Indexes

About the Author

Flora Joy received her bachelor's, master's, and doctoral degrees all in the field of communication and education. She began teaching elementary reading and language arts in Knox County, Tennessee, in the early 1960s. Shortly thereafter she was hired by East Tennessee State University (ETSU) in Johnson City, Tennessee, where she is currently a professor emeritus in the Storytelling Division of the Department of Curriculum and Instruction.

Flora Joy has been described as a "founder" in the world of storytelling. Some of the following are examples:

- The master's degree program in storytelling on the campus of ETSU, one of the most unique graduate education experiences in the world

- *Storytelling World,* an international, fully refereed journal for which she has served as editor since its first issue in the 1980s

- The National Storytelling Youth Olympics—an event that gives prestigious attention to young tellers

- The Annual Multicultural Storytelling Cruise (that journeys around the world to study storytelling practices both at home and abroad)

- The International Storytelling Institutes—an annual event for in-depth study of storytelling

- The Annual Storytelling Resource Awards Program that involves all English-language publications in storytelling.

Flora has a multitude of publications to her credit and has won many prestigious awards, including the State Teacher of the Year (for Tennessee), the Outstanding Teaching and Outstanding Service awards at ETSU, and the Lifetime Achievement Award given by the National Storytelling Network.

To Flora, though, her storytelling work is merely beginning.